W9-BCR-762
SEP 1980
RECEIVED
OHIO DOMINICAN
COLLEGE LIBRARY
COLUMBUS, OHIO
43219

Twayne's English Authors Series

EDITOR OF THIS VOLUME

Herbert Sussman

Northeastern University

Mrs. Humphry Ward

TEAS 288

MRS. HUMPHRY WARD

By ESTHER MARIAN GREENWELL SMITH

Polk Community College

TWAYNE PUBLISHERS

A DIVISION OF G. K. HALL & CO., BOSTON

Published in 1980 by Twayne Publishers,
A Division of G. K. Hall & Co.

First Printing

Library of Congress Cataloging in Publication Data

Smith, Esther Marian Greenwell.
Mrs. Humphry Ward.

(Twayne's English authors series ; TEAS 288)
Bibliography: p. 155-59
Includes index.
1. Ward, Mary Augusta Arnold, 1851-1920—Criticism and interpretation.
PR5717.S6 823'.8 79-24476
ISBN 0-8057-6766-5

To my husband,
Elton Edward Smith,
Professor, University of South Florida, whose faith in
me initiated and sustained my study of Mrs. Humphry Ward

Contents

About the Author

Dr. Esther Marian Greenwell Smith is a professor of English at Polk Community College, Winter Haven, Florida. She has taught at Portland State College, Portland, Oregon, and at Florida Southern College, Lakeland, Florida, and at high schools in Oregon and New York. She has published children's fiction and collaborated with her husband, Dr. Elton Edward Smith, in a study of *William Godwin.*

Preface

Two questions are posed by Mrs. Humphry Ward's great popularity during her lifetime and virtual oblivion since: How accurately did she speak to and for her age? What is her artistic merit? Her success with both the reading public and many critics (even those who disapproved of her religious convictions could not ignore her works) from 1888 to 1920 answers in part the first question. Further evidence is given by such scholars as the Englishman J. Stuart Walters, who in 1912 wrote that no literary personality had made a deeper impression on his day, and the Frenchman Abel Chevalley, who wrote in 1925 that it would be very difficult to understand the England of the end of the nineteenth century without recourse to Mrs. Ward's works.

The question of her artistic merit is harder to answer and more important to her continued significance. William Dean Howells, in *Heroines of Fiction* (1901), considered her not quite but almost the equal of George Eliot; but William Lyon Phelps, in *Essays on Modern Novelists* (1921), thought it was time someone protested her vogue; and Lionel Stevenson, in *The English Novel: a Panorama* (1960), judged her deficient in humor and incapable of creating living characters. Yet even her severest critics concede that she was a consistent aand above-average craftsman.

The bulk of her works demands a leisure seldom enjoyed by modern readers; and the carefully balanced romance and realism, progress and tradition, conflict and optimism that are characteristic of the intellectual and social milieu she represents are untenable in a world that has discarded many Victorian concepts. However, her recreation of real or composite personalities is effective, moving, and memorable, and she occasionally touches the universal themes of human relationships with the insight of an artist. The following study endeavors to view the total work and to find the rare moments.

Since her fame was initiated by *Robert Elsmere,* a novel

presenting the leading religious issue of her day—revealed dogma versus evolutionary humanism—the emphasis on, or absence of, current issues seemed a useful basis for the analytical organization of her twenty-five novels. Accordingly, the first chapter traces the background and personal experiences out of which Mrs. Ward wrote. The second chapter deals with her religiously oriented works. The third chapter discusses her five novels of social concern. The fourth chapter presents the twelve novels in which no issues seriously compete with romance. The fifth chapter combines her nonfiction writing on World War I, her war novels, and her unfinished autobiography.

The final chapter presents a cross section of critical reaction to her writing since the appearance of *Robert Elsmere* in 1888, and an attempt to predict her continuing significance. The background for her involvement in the religious, social, and war issues is adequately documented, and recent scholarship has uncovered some facets of her personal life that throw light on her creative process and the reality behind her Victorian gentility. However, the sincerity of her convictions, the validity of her insights, and the effectiveness of her artistry must remain a matter for critical analysis and public rediscovery or neglect.

ESTHER MARIAN GREENWELL SMITH

Lakeland, Florida

Chronology

1851 Mary Augusta Arnold born June 11, Tasmania, Australia; first of the eight children of Thomas Arnold and Julia Sorrell.

1854 Thomas Arnold becomes a Catholic and forfeits his position as school administrator.

1856 Family returns to England, where Thomas secures employment under John Henry Newman at the Catholic University in Dublin; Mary spends most of her time with Arnold relatives at Fox How.

1858 Attends Miss Anne Clough's school for two years.

1860 Miss Davies's school at Shiffnal in Shropshire.

1862 Father moves to Newman's Oratory School, Birmingham.

1864 Miss May's school near Clifton.

1865 Father returns to the Anglican Church and moves to Oxford to teach.

1867 Mary comes to Oxford, begins independent study in the Bodleian.

1869 First work, "A Westmoreland Story," accepted for the *Churchman's Companion.*

1870 Uncle, William Edward Forster, presents the Education Bill.

1871 Engaged to T. Humphry Ward, fellow and tutor of Brasenose College, Oxford. "A Morning in the Bodleian," essay, privately printed. Declines invitation to write a volume on Spain for the historical series edited by Edward Freeman.

1872 Married, April 6, by Dean Arthur Stanley, biographer of her grandfather; begins nine years' residence in Oxford. Article on *Poema del Cid, MacMillan's Magazine;* both Wards contribute to *Saturday Review* and *Oxford Spectator.*

1874 Daughter, Dorothy, born. Serves as secretary to the committee securing Lectures for Women at Oxford.

1876 Son, Arnold, born. Thomas Arnold reconverts to Catholicism, rejoins Newman; Julia stays in Oxford.
1877 Begins writing articles on early Spanish ecclesiastics and kings for the *Dictionary of Christian Biography.* The Committee for Lectures for Women becomes the Association for the Education of Women.
1878 Founding of first women's hall of residence at Oxford.
1879 Daughter, Janet, born.
1880 *Milly and Olly* published. Mr. Ward accepts a post on the *Times.* Visits William E. Forster, Chief Secretary for Ireland.
1881 *Unbelief and Sin, a Protest Addressed to Those Who Attended the Bampton Lecture of Sunday March 6,* printed anonymously. Moves to London; completes work for the *Dictionary of Christian Biography;* begins feature articles and reviews of Spanish, French, and American books for *MacMillan's.* Writes weekly articles for the *Church Guardian* and the *Oxford Chronicle.*
1883 Gertrude Ward, sister-in-law, comes to live with them; serves as secretary for eight years.
1884 *Miss Bretherton* published.
1885 Julia Arnold, her sister, marries Leonard Huxley. Translation of *Journal Intime of Henri Frederic Amiel* published.
1888 *Robert Elsmere* appears, February 26; her mother, Julia, dies, April. William Gladstone writes "*Robert Elsmere* and the Battle of Belief" for the May *Nineteenth Century.*
1889 Answer: "The New Reformation, a Dialogue," in January *Nineteenth Century.*
1890 *The History of David Grieve.* Purchases Stocks; suffers mysterious internal pain and nervous crippling.
1893 Passmore Edwards Settlement planned.
1894 *Marcella.* A paper for Unitarians delivered at Essex Hall, Norwich.
1895 *The Story of Bessie Costrell.*
1896 *Sir George Tressady,* serialized in *Century Magazine,* then a book. Miss Bessie Churcher comes to be secretary and remains the rest of her life.
1897 Passmore Edwards Settlement opens; lecture on "The Peasant in Literature," in Glasgow.
1898 *Helbeck of Bannisdale.*
1899 Establishes Invalid Children's Schools. Writes preface for

Smith and Elder's Haworth edition of the Brontë novels.

1900 *Eleanor,* serialized in *Harper's Magazine,* then a book. Father, Thomas Arnold, dies.

1902 Dramatization of *Eleanor.*

1903 *Lady Rose's Daughter.* Janet engaged to Macaulay Trevelyan.

1904 Janet marries. William Arnold, her favorite brother, dies.

1905 *The Marriage of William Ashe.*

1906 *Fenwick's Career.*

1908 *The Testing of Diana Mallory.* Visits the United States and Canada; entertained by President Theodore Roosevelt.

1909 *Daphne,* or *Marriage à la Mode.*

1910 *Lady Merton, Colonist,* or *Canadian Born.* Helps elect her son as Unionist candidate from West Herts Division.

1911 *The Case of Richard Meynell.*

1912 Active in the antisuffragist movement.

1913 *The Mating of Lydia. The Coryston Family.*

1914 *Delia Blanchflower.*

1915 *Eltham House.* Theodore Roosevelt asks her to write about England's part in the war.

1916 Official visits to war centers reported in *Letters to an American Friend;* published through syndicated press; then as *England's Effort. A Great Success. Lady Connie.*

1917 Second visit to war zones reported in *Towards the Goal. "Missing".*

1918 *A Writer's Recollections. The War and Elizabeth,* or *Elizabeth's Campaign.*

1919 *Fields of Victory. Cousin Philip* or *Helene.* Sells Grosvenor Place, August 29; visits the Lake District for the last time, in September. Ill at Christmas.

1920 Chosen one of the first seven women magistrates of England; honorary doctorate, University of Edinburgh. Mr. Ward emergency surgery, March 11; she suffering from bronchitis; dies March 24. *Harvest* published posthumously.

CHAPTER 1

Her Heritage and Experiences

ROBERT *Elsmere* made its debut on February 26, 1888. Nine days later its appearance was recognized by the *Scotsman* and the *Morning Post*. Twelve days after its first sales the *British Weekly* "wept over it"; a week later the *Academy* compared it to George Eliot's *Adam Bede*. In the next ten days the *Manchester Guardian* gave it two columns; the *Saturday* reviewed it; and Walter Pater wrote, in the *Church Guardian*, that it was "a *chef d'oeuvre* of that kind of quiet evolution of character through circumstance, introduced into English literature by Miss Austen and carried to perfection in France by George Sand."[1] In May, the *Nineteenth Century* published the most famous of hundreds of reactions—William Gladstone's "*Robert Elsmere* and the Battle of Belief." Mrs. Humphry Ward, née Mary Augusta Arnold, had achieved rank as a spokesman for her times—a position she held until her death in 1920.

That Mary Ward should write something worthy of public acclaim was no surprise to her friends. Granddaughter of Dr. Thomas Arnold of Rugby, niece of Matthew Arnold the poet and critic, and at twenty a recognized scholar of early Spanish history, Mary Augusta Arnold had been writing for publication since 1869 when her "A Westmoreland Story" was accepted for publication by Charlotte Yonge, editor of the *Churchman's Companion*. And although her plan of study was almost entirely self-directed (no women students were admitted to Oxford for another decade), Mary Arnold worked at the Bodleian Library at Oxford from 1867 to 1871 so effectively that John Richard Green, the historian, unhesitatingly recommended her to Edward Freeman as the best person to write a volume on Spain for the historical series Freeman was editing. She could not accept Mr. Freeman's invitation because she was deeply involved with plans for her marriage to Mr. Humphry Ward,

Fellow and Tutor of Brasenose College. But when, in 1877, Dean Wace asked her to join the scholars writing for the *Dictionary of Christian Biography,* she began the disciplined study that was to produce almost two hundred articles, from a few lines to eight pages in length, on the leaders of the West Goths in Spain during the fifth, sixth, and seventh centuries.

I *The Battle of Faith*

The effect of her work in early church history is clearly portrayed in the novel *Robert Elsmere* when the hero discovers that, because of his study in historical criticism, he can no longer accept the orthodox beliefs appropriate to his position. The popularity of the novel testified to the fact that a similar religious drama was taking place on a national scale. When Mary Arnold was born in 1851, England had been feeling the repercussions of the Tractarian Movement (now generally known as the Oxford Movement) for almost twenty years. It was precipitated by a famous sermon on "National Apostasy," preached by John Keble, at Oxford, on July 14, 1833. In the years that followed, Keble, John Henry Newman, and Hurrell Froude propagandized tirelessly for reaffirmation of doctrines that would strengthen the Established Church. One cause for their alarm was the several acts of Parliament that seemed to them to jeopardize the concept of a National Church. The Act of 1829 had emancipated the Roman Catholics; the Reform Bill of 1832 had enlarged the electorate to include Dissenters, and a bill in 1833 proposed to suppress ten bishoprics of the Irish Protestant Church, which was regarded at the time as an integral part of the Church of England. But their chief concern was the spiritual apathy of both the clergy and the laity of the Established Church, an apathy that fed the cause of Dissent.

Their chief vehicle was *Tracts for the Times,* published in pamphlet form from 1833 to 1841, and stressing the Church Catholic and Apostolic. By 1839, Newman, who wrote most of the tracts, found himself questioning the justification of his own position outside the Roman Church. Two years later, in the ninetieth and the last of the Tracts, this leader of the High Church movement stated his position so boldly that the hitherto academic controversy became a matter for ecclesiastical action, and Newman and his followers were placed under official stigma.

In 1842 Newman withdrew from Oxford, and three years later he was admitted to the Roman Catholic Church. Only a few of the Tractarians followed Newman, but the whole High Church wing of the Anglican Church had been aroused to a new zeal. After his ordination in Rome, Newman served the Roman Church in several ways, but his two outstanding contributions were his work to establish a Catholic university in Dublin and his book *Apologia pro Vita Sua* (1864), which told the story of his spiritual ordeal so effectively that it changed most of the public opinion toward him as a man, if not toward his theological position.

Early in this battle of faith, Newman's best known critic was Mary Ward's grandfather, Dr. Thomas Arnold. This famous English educator and progenitor of an illustrious clan of intellectual Englishmen was born in 1795, son of William Arnold, a collector of customs. After graduation from Oxford, Thomas Arnold spent eight years teaching, studying, and tutoring. During this time, he came under the influence of German literature and also developed the personality for which he is best remembered, a personality shaped by a vivid experience of the reality of Jesus Christ, a reality reflected in every spiritual, moral, intellectual, and emotional act of his life. In 1827 he was chosen headmaster of Rugby. By treating the boys with confidence and by impressing upon them his own sense of the value of knowledge and the sacredness of duty, he regenerated Rugby and influenced public-school education throughout England.

Arnold's course was not always an untroubled one; in some ways his record of highminded nonconformity foreshadowed the militant idealism of his granddaughter. In 1829 he published a pamphlet on the *Christian Duty of Conceding the Roman Catholic Claims,* in which he ruthlessly exposed the incompetence of the clergy as a body to deal with such questions. The attendance at Rugby was hurt by this and other outspoken criticisms of the clergy. When the dominant party at Oxford attempted, in 1836, to keep Dr. Renn Dickson Hampden from a professorship on the grounds of alleged heresy, Arnold's unsigned article in the *Edinburgh Review* brought a formal request from the trustees concerning the article's authorship and a vote of censure that almost passed. In this and other articles, Dr. Arnold led the Broad Church spokesmen (those who advocated a tolerant and comprehensive approach to doctrine) in attacking the Tractarians as preaching a return to superstition and popery, a revival of the judaizing spirit condemned by Saint Paul. However, when Arnold returned to Oxford in 1841, as Regius Professor of History, he was cordially received, for Newman was under official censure and Arnold's Broad Church attitude was recognized as hostility to anything that seemed to retard the extension of Christ's Church.

Suddenly, on June 12, 1842, on the last day of his forty-seventh year, Dr. Arnold died of an attack of angina pectoris, leaving his dedication to a reverent faith and independent thought to the vicissitudes of history. The eldest of his nine children, Jane, was twenty-one, and the youngest, Frances, was eight. Matthew and Thomas Arnold, nineteen and eighteen at the time of their father's death, were students at Oxford during Newman's troubled years there. Matthew went occasionally to hear Newman preach because of his remarkable power with words. Thomas, who heard Newman only once, found his mannerisms offensive. The brothers, their friend Arthur Hugh Clough, and a few other kindred spirits were absorbed at the time with the diverse philosophical worlds of George Sand, Ralph Waldo Emerson, and Thomas Carlyle.

Five years after the death of Dr. Arnold, and two years after Newman's admission to the Catholic Church, young Thomas Arnold was graduated from Oxford with honors. He quickly secured a position in the Colonial Office; but speculative liberalism, humanitarianism, and his own spiritual quest sent him, in 1847, to New Zealand, the land of hope and brotherhood, as a homesteader. Matthew Arnold, in his Oxford lecture on Celtic literature, identified Celtic traits as imagination, rebellion against fact, spirituality, a tendency to dream, charm, unworldliness, a passionate love of beauty, and ineffectualness in practical matters; Thomas Arnold seems to have been a winsome but heartbreaking assortment of these traits. His impracticality was soon demonstrated, even to himself, when he endeavored to clear land with his own hands. He resisted the first opportunity for escape, a secretaryship to Sir George Grey, governor of the colony; but another year of physical labor dimmed the flame of his intellectual idealism, and he accepted the offer of the new governor of Australia, Sir William Denison, to organize the primary education of that land. Whatever sense of defeat he felt was soon lost in the joy of congenial work and in his engagement to the beautiful Julia Sorell, granddaughter of one of the first governors of Tasmania.

Mrs. Ward said of her mother's family that they were French Huguenots who had settled in England in 1685. A recent biographer, Enid Huws Jones, labels this "foreign" strain, manifested by "delicate features, small, beautifully shaped hands and feet, . . .vivacity and quickness and overflowing energy, "[2] Spanish.[3] Mrs. Ward felt her mother's Protestantism was not so much a spiritual matter as the instinct of strong individualism, a basic tenet of Mrs. Ward's response to religion. Julia's horror of Catholicism was real, so real that just before her wedding she made Thomas promise never to become a Roman Catholic. But by a process he could never adequately explain, Thomas came under the spell of the *Tracts* that came into his hands in Tasmania, and the spiritual drama of England became the painfully personal drama of Thomas's family. Nevertheless, Julia remained loving and loyal, determined not to repeat her family history. Her grandfather had left his wife and his children and a distinguished career in the Cold Stream Guards to live with another officer's wife. He had been banished—or promoted—to the governorship of Van Diemen's Land (later Tasmania). And Julia's mother had left her three daughters at boarding school in England to go off with a young officer.

When in October 1854 Thomas Arnold was received into the Church of Rome at Hobart, Tasmania, neither the colony nor his wife could quite believe that a son of Dr. Arnold had taken such a step. But the colony moved quickly to end his influence on their education. Mary was five years old; her brothers William and Theodore, four and one, when the family returned to England and the generous kindness of Arnold relatives. Mary remembered being met by William E. Forster, whose wife, Jane Arnold, was her godmother, and then going to Fox How, the Arnold home in Westmoreland, presided over with unfailing graciousness by Dr. Arnold's widow. Thomas accepted educational work under Newman, in Dublin, and later in Birmingham, at the oratory to which Newman had been sent when his impractical ways became a handicap to the Dublin university. Because the Thomas Arnold family grew in numbers but not in income, Mary became the welcome charge of her grandmother and Aunt Frances. And since, according to the custom of that day in religiously divided families, the sons were trained in their father's faith and the daughters, in their mother's, Mary was never exposed to Catholic teaching as were her brothers. But she sensed the heartache her grandmother knew at the thought of

Newman "examining" Dr. Arnold's grandsons; and she came to feel that her mother's struggles with poverty, even her own childish privations, were somehow Newman's fault rather than her father's. The intellectual, refined, serviceable qualities of her grandfather's religion, so beautifully exemplified at Fox How and in the lives of all the Arnold aunts and uncles, were to characterize her sincere religious convictions throughout her life.

However, like George Eliot, Mary Arnold had an Evangelical phase. While at the Rock Terrace School for Young Ladies, at Shiffnal, Shropshire, Mary fell headlong in love with the Vicar of Shiffnal and his gentle Evangelical wife. Janet Trevelyan describes her mother's girlish infatuation: "Going to church—especially in the evenings, when the Vicar preached—became a romance; seeing Mrs. Cunliffe pass by in her pony-carriage lent a radiance to the day."[4]

Many of the people and places Mary Arnold knew during these early years appear in her novels. Her dark and light hours at Shiffnal are recounted as the background for the heroine of *Marcella.* Her godmother, Mrs. Forster, is seen in the mature Marcella of *Sir George Tressady.* The hills and lakes of Fox How appear in *Fenwick's Career* and *"Missing."* But of greatest importance to the future author of *Robert Elsmere* was her father's decision in June 1865 to return to the Anglican Church. Mary was fourteen, home for her long holiday, when her father first showed her Oxford University, for friends who had welcomed his change of faith had promptly secured for him tutoring at the university. In the eleven years he remained there, he produced a *Manual on English Literature* and became an authority in Early English.

Mary came home to Oxford to stay when she was sixteen. Although as the eldest of eight children she was needed to help her mother a great deal of the time, and although she was keenly aware of the family's financial difficulties, this period was a happy one for Mary. She helped her father with his research, studied piano to good account, and met many important and charming people. Among them was Mark Pattison, rector of Lincoln, whose early years had been dominated by Newman, but who now led the liberal party that fought year after year to liberalize the religious requirements for degrees at Oxford University; he not only made the shy but brilliant girl welcome in his home but sent her to the Bodleian Library with the counsel, "Get to the bottom of something." Her reading in the dogmatic church records of fifth- and sixth-century Spain and the critical German commentaries of the eighteenth century led her to agreement with Benjamin Jowett that the Gospels, like other historical records, must be understood as products of their culture and the uncritical historical sense of their writers. Like Robert Elsmere, she became convinced that miracles did not happen in the nineteenth century and that their supposed happening in the first century could be explained by the credulity of the people of that day. Nevertheless, like her uncle Matthew Arnold, whose *Essays in Criticism* (1865) profoundly influenced her, she believed that the Church of England was intrinsically at the center of the best of England's culture—its best schools, its greatest buildings, the coronation of its monarchs, its social structure, its literature, even its tax structure.

II *Apprenticeship*

But Mary's time was not totally given to study. In a university town with a scarcity of eligible young women available to make up proper dinner parties, Mary's good looks and intelligence were in demand. At some such function she met Thomas Humphry Ward, son of the Rev. Henry Ward, member of a Hull ship-owning family who missed their chance at fortune when sail gave way to steam. Until his ordination at thirty, Henry Ward seems to have lived the life of a country gentleman, addicted to hunting and shooting. He would have liked a Mayfair parish but accepted the industrial suburbs of Finsbury. His wife, Jane Sandwith, was the daughter of a physician; one of her brothers was a notable surgeon, traveler, and Wesleyan. Jane Ward died at forty-two, having borne seventeen children, twelve of whom grew up. Henry Ward found difficulty in maintaining a proper standard of living for such a family but made matters worse by unsuccessful speculation. Humphry, their third surviving child, retained an enthusiasm for shooting, but he distinguished himself with a First in Greats and a love of art that eventually led to a distinguished career as an art critic for the *Times.*

In May 1871 Mary Arnold and Humphry Ward became engaged. Humphry's first duty was to secure permission from his principal to marry, since marriage for Fellows had just been made a possibility. This permission secured, he visited his father and again received approval. Then he made the acquaintance of the Arnolds with an idyllic visit to Fox How and the Lake Country. By September he was house hunting, and the diary that gives tantalizing glimpses of the period dwindled and stopped. On April 6, 1872, Mary Arnold, not yet twenty-one, became Mrs. Humphry Ward, and the couple began their nine years' residency in Oxford as neighbors of Walter Pater. During the busy days of preparation for her marriage, Mary had produced the essay "A Morning in Bodleian." Shortly after her marriage her article on the *Poema del Cid* appeared in *Macmillan's Magazine*, and both the Wards contributed regularly to *Saturday Review* and *Oxford Spectator*. She dreamed of writing a history of Spain, and in this and several attempts at fiction she was encouraged and criticized by J. R. Green, who counseled her to learn to write by writing, and who let her try her hand at a primer of English literature which was actually completed by Stopford Brooke. Mary's problem was that she wrote twenty pages on Beowulf alone; at such a rate the primer would have become a massive volume.

In 1874 their first child, Dorothy Mary, was born. Mary also undertook the time-consuming task of serving as secretary to the committee securing Lectures for Women at Oxford, the first of her impressive contributions to the betterment of the world through education that was the central conviction of her faith. She also enjoyed a Christmas vacation in Paris, where she met such notable members of the historical-religious controversy as Ernest Renan (1823–92), author of *Vie de Jésus*, and Hippolyte Adolphe Taine (1828–93), French historian, critic, and leader of the nineteenth century "cult of science," and the famous hostess Madame Mohl (née Mary Clarke, 1793–1883), an English woman educated in France, whose receptions in the Rue de Bac for nearly forty years attracted many famous intellectuals. The Wards also saw Sarah Bernhardt perform. These experiences would later furnish details and concepts for some of her novels.

The year 1876 was to bring the joy of the birth of a son, Arnold Sandwith, and the sorrow of mysterious and painful experiences for her parents. On the very eve of his election to the professorship of Early English, her father returned to the Catholic Church. "Pupils no longer came to be taught by a professing Catholic, and Julia [his wife] was reduced to taking 'boarders' in a smaller house in Church Walk, while Tom earned what he could by incessant writing and eventually took work again at the Catholic University in Dublin."[5] However, this time Julia did not go with him, but stayed in Oxford; not only could her sense of wifely duty not cope with her husband's return to a faith she hated, but it was now apparent that she had cancer. Her poverty and suffering came to an end in 1888. Mary sought lovingly to be true to both parents.

In 1877 Mary accepted the invitation of Dean Wace, general editor of *The Dictionary of Christian Biography,* to write the items on early Spanish ecclesiastics and kings. At the same time, the Committee for Lectures for Women expanded to the Association for the Education of Women, work that culminated in the founding of the first women's hall of residence at Oxford, in 1878. The following year, 1879, the last of her children was born, Janet Penrose. In 1880, she visited her uncle William Forster while he was serving as Chief Secretary for Ireland at one of the worst periods of the Irish land-war. The suffering and tension she saw there was relieved by a visit to the Westmoreland country with her two older children and the writing of a fictionalized account of the visit, *Milly and Olly.* But the major event of the year was Mr. Ward's acceptance of a post on the *Times.* He was assigned to write political articles, plus other items of interest to him. Later he became art critic, a position he held for twenty-five years.

During the winter of 1880–81, the family stayed in Oxford while Mr. Ward "tried out" London. It was on March 6, 1881, a Sunday, that an incident occurred that occasioned Mrs. Ward's first publication in the battle of faith: she attended the first Bampton lecture of the Reverend Mr. John Wordsworth and heard him castigate the holders of unorthodox religious views as committers of a grievous sin. Not only did this dogmatic assault strike at her own convictions, but it also maligned the noble lives of such men as Thomas Hill Green, Benjamin Jowett, and her uncle, Matthew Arnold. A few days later there appeared in the window of Slatter & Rose an anonymous pamphlet entitled *Unbelief and Sin, A Protest Addressed to Those Who Attended the Bampton Lecture of Sunday, March 6.* Written in the form of a dialogue between two Oxford men, the work sold well until a certain ecclesiastic pointed out to the bookseller that, since it bore no printer's name, it was illegal. Furthermore, this conservative dignitary made it clear that he would take steps to prosecute the bookseller if the offending liberal pamphlet continued on sale. The bookseller hurriedly returned the unsold copies to Mrs. Ward, who submitted good-humoredly and sent the remaining pamphlets to her friends.

In November 1881 the family moved to a comfortable old house in Russell Square, Bloomsbury. Built in 1745, the house had a small garden and many little powder-closets, one of which Mrs. Ward appropriated as her writing-room. Her work on the *Dictionary of Christian Biography* was almost finished, but she increasingly contributed articles to the *Times:* articles on Spanish novels, American novels, Tennyson, the death of Anthony Trollope, and reviews of books on Christian origins. She was also writing a weekly article for the *Church Guardian* and contributing to the *Oxford Chronicle.* When Mr. John Morley, editor of the *Pall Mall Gazette,* to which she had contributed numerous articles, became editor of *Macmillan Magazine,* he made the flattering request that she write a monthly article. Between February 1883 and June 1885 she wrote twelve such articles, including in her range of subjects the young Spanish Romanticist Gustavo Becquer, John Keats, Jane Austen, and a review of Walter Pater's *Marius the Epicurean.* In the meantime, Mr. Ward not only wrote for the *Times* but continued to edit *Ward's Poets,* the first three volumes of which had been published by Macmillan in 1880. The 1883 edition covered poets from Chaucer to Rossetti. Nineteen editions of "The English Poets" appeared in Ward's lifetime; the fourth volume, from Browning to Rupert Brooke, came out as late as 1918. In such a busily writing family, the arrival of Mr. Ward's sister Gertrude, an honors graduate of Somerville Hall, the women's residence Mrs. Ward had helped to establish at Oxford, was a welcome assistance; she served as Mrs. Ward's secretary for eight years.

Mary's brother Willie, who had joined the staff of the *Manchester Guardian,* was a frequent visitor, and her illustrious uncle Matthew Arnold was occasionally to be caught for an evening. The Wards' work and their ties to such people as William Forster and Matthew Arnold secured for them a place in the literary and political circles of England. In 1885 Mrs. Ward wrote to a friend of attending the wedding of Alfred Lyttelton and Laura Tennant, at which Mr. William Gladstone, uncle of the groom, gave the breakfast speech. In the same year Mrs. Ward's sister Julia married Leonard Huxley, son of Thomas Huxley, the well-known scientist, educator, and social critic.

Despite her demanding social obligations, Mary Ward was laboring faithfully with the translation of the outstanding work of Swiss mysticism, *Journal Intime of Henri Frederic Amiel,* begun in 1884 and published in 1885. This work was interrupted by an occasion pregnant with two novels. In 1884, she invited to tea the twenty-three-year-old American actress Mary Anderson, whose beauty was the talk of London. The guests included another American, Henry James. After the tea, and dinner, James and the Wards were the guests of Miss Anderson at her new play, *Comedy and Tragedy,* by Gilbert. The performance was a disappointment, with the actress guilty of excesses in all her expressions. A few days later, Mrs. Ward told her sister-in-law that she had a full-length story in mind, combining her new insight into acting and comments Henry James had made at the dinner table on spontaneity versus training. *Miss Bretherton* was written in six weeks in the summer of 1884; Henry James's novel *The Tragic Muse* appeared in 1888.

III *Fame*

Late in 1884 she began work on *Robert Elsmere;* the first chapters were rejected by Macmillan but accepted by George Smith of Smith, Elder & Co., with an advance of £200. The novel was finished in 1887, with much cutting, and made its dramatic appearance on February 24, 1888, just six weeks before the death of her mother, Julia Arnold. Much of the comment that came from pulpit and critics she chose to ignore, but after a pleasant but inconclusive visit with Mr. Gladstone on the issues of the novel, and the appearance of his article "*Robert Elsmere* and the Battle of Belief," in the May issue of *Nineteenth Century,* she decided to defend her position. "The New Reformation, a Dialogue" appeared in the January 1889 issue of *Nineteenth Century.* Furthermore, she determined to prove the effectiveness of the "new" religion, beginning work for a settlement at University Hall, Gordon Square. She also announced her next novel, *The History of David Grieve,* the American and Canadian rights of which were sold to Macmillan for £7,000.

She paid a heavy price for her strenuous efforts, suffering a mysterious internal pain and nervous crippling of her right leg.

There were other "burdens"; Gertrude had long dreamed of being a missionary nurse in Zanzibar, sent out by her own very orthodox church, St. John's. She had found the "heresies" of *Robert Elsmere* as hard to live with as had the hero's saintly wife, Catherine, and, despite Mrs. Ward's refusal to see the rightness of her dream, late in the afternoon of New Year's Day 1891, Gertrude left 61 Russell Square to begin her years of training. The preceding summer Dorothy had become sixteen; on her fell the cares of Gertrude—a relationship to her mother that she carried gladly for the rest of her life.

The success of *Robert Elsmere* had made possible the building of Lower Grayswood, in Surrey; with the success of *David Grieve* assured in 1892, the Wards leased Stocks, near Tring, for £400 a year. Later they bought Stocks and enlarged its estate, selling Lower Grayswood, for both Humphry and Mary were working strenuously to maintain their professional and social position. Somehow Mrs. Ward managed to spearhead the planning of the Passmore Edwards Settlement, writing the letters and presenting the lectures that secured the funds the project demanded, at the same time that she completed the last of her three-volume novels, *Marcella* (1894), the short, untypical novel *The Story of Bessie Costrell* (1895), and the first of her serialized novels, *Sir George Tressady* (1896). Fortunately Miss Bessie Churcher came to be her secretary in 1896—and stayed the rest of her life. The Passmore Edwards Settlement, Tavistock Place, Bloomsbury, London, opened on October 10, 1897.

The Settlement House, since renamed Mary Ward House (or Centre) and still serving its community, was designed to uplift the young people of the area by attractive surroundings, cultural and philosophical lectures, and refining activities. Not all of the residents and young adult visitors found this program appealing, but the growing effort to serve the children of the area was a marked success. It was a common practice to lock children out of their living quarters when their mothers went to work, for fear that they might start fires. Mrs. Ward decided that adults did not need the settlement before eight o'clock but the children did. As soon as the schools closed, the children gathered at the settlement for warmth and play. This was the origin of the evening play-center movement in London. Both Dorothy and Janet were pressed into service and learned, as did most of the workers, by trial and error how to help their eager but unruly patrons. By 1900 the weekly attendance was close to two thousand. And when these dedicated women realized the needs of the hot, bored, quarrelsome children that swarmed the area in the holiday month of August, they opened their gardens and began vacation school. Even Miss Churcher added the organization of the holiday school to her other work. But the most dramatic contribution to education came early in 1899 when the Passmore Edwards School for Invalid Children was opened. Many humanitarians had been calling attention to the plight of these unfortunate ones. In 1893 the London School Board knew of over eight hundred children who could not attend the schools provided for them because of physical handicaps. There were probably twice that number. And even if they could have been furnished transportation, most of them could not have survived in the rough and tumble of the Spartan schools of the day. Many of these children were left, sometimes for fourteen hours a day, cold, inadequately fed, and without any mental stimulus. With a combination of charity and public support, crippled children were brought to school facilities altered to fit their needs and provided not only education but hot meals and special attention. The school was used until 1960.

Amid such Herculean activities, Mrs. Ward still found time to supervise her son's education, at Eton then Oxford, and her daughters' activities and clothing. The family had been forced to move from Russell Square, as the land was needed for the building of the first Imperial Hotel. Their new address was "better" than Bloomsbury, 25 Grosvenor Place on the edge of Belgravia, just over the way from the gardens of Buckingham Palace. There were refreshing excursions to Italy, informative trips into the north-country for settings and appropriate characters. There were friendships developed with such social reformers as Beatrice and Sydney Webb and such generous aristocrats as the Duke and Duchess of Bedford. She still had forty or more callers at her Thursdays and gave dinner parties that included famous writers, government officials, and church dignitaries. And her books appeared at one- two-, or three-year intervals: *Helbeck of Bannisdale* in 1898; *Eleanor* in 1900; *Lady Rose's Daughter* in 1903; *The Marriage of William Ashe* in 1905; and *Fenwick's Career* in 1906.

In 1904 Janet married George Macaulay Trevelyan. In 1908 Mrs. Ward visited the United States and Canada, with mixed results. She was widely acclaimed and graciously received in both countries, but she responded with quite different attitudes. *Daphne*, or *Marriage à la Mode*, which appeared in 1909, is a bitter attack on the American divorce laws seen as an offense against the Anglican church; *Lady Merton, Colonist*, or *Canadian Born*, which appeared in 1910, is a paean to the beauty and virtues of Canada as part of the British Empire. But one American did win her friendship, President Theodore Roosevelt, who entertained her at the White House. In 1915 he wrote to her asking that she inform America of the great effort England was expending in the war; her response was *Letters to an American Friend*, open letters published in American newspapers through a syndicated press, later in book form as *England's Effort* (1916). Many felt that she did contribute to the decision that took America into the war on the side of the Allies. For this and her second book on the subject, *Towards the Goal* (1917), she was given approval from the War Ministry to visit off-limits military installations and the front, making her one of the first "official" woman war correspondents and proving not only the esteem in which her talents were held but the dedication with which, even at sixty-five, she sought to use those talents for her country's good.

Despite her patriotism (so blatantly expressed in the last of her war commentaries, *Fields of Victory*, 1919) and her pride in her accomplishments, Mrs. Ward did not believe in women's suffrage. Many of her friends and relatives did, and she was active in aiding her son Arnold to win a seat in Parliament, for West Hertfordshire, in 1909, but she had an instinctive dislike of the public display that the suffragists practiced and that she saw as essential to political life. She saw women's role as that fulfilled by all the charming hostesses of salons and dinners at which much of the real work of legislative power was done, as she had portrayed such women in *Marcella* and *Lady Rose's Daughter*, and their "ugly" counterparts in *The Coryston Family* (1913) and *Delia Blanchflower* (1914). She was essentially a shy person, with feminine interests and sweetness, who suffered her fame and public appeals for causes she believed in. And although she made considerable demands upon those about her—for her often ailing body or assistance in her work—the details of her personal life were discreetly masked in both her social world and her writing.

Consequently, the greatest heartache of her life was little

known until recently, and critics sometimes condemned the apparent shallowness of her work with the argument that she had known too much success, too little suffering. How deeply she felt the suffering she saw in her family and elsewhere is debatable, but the failure of her only son seems to have cut so deeply that Janet Trevelyan, in her biography of her mother, mentions Arnold as an adult only indirectly, when his mother assisted him in winning a seat in Parliament. Arnold Ward was a quiet but brilliant child who, like his father, became a fine cricketeer and a master of Greek versification. He was a Scholar of Baliol, Newcastle Scholar, Craven Scholar, Chancellor's Prizeman, and Double First, and became a *Times* correspondent in Egypt, Sudan, and India. He was called to the bar in 1903 and in 1909 won a seat in Parliament. He never married, and during the war his work was characterized by much enforced idleness which led to compulsive gambling. The villagers about Stocks and perceptive friends sensed that some of Mrs. Ward's late writing was done not only to offset the deprivations of war but to pay "Arnie's" debts. Certainly some of her late writing is uninspired, although occasionally she catches the tones of hope and fear that echoed through those war-torn years.

In the summer of 1919 the Wards sold Grosvenor Place, their London house; in the fall they visited the Lake District for the last time. At Christmas Mrs. Ward was ill and recovered so slowly that she could not enjoy the honorary degree awarded her by the University of Edinburgh or the distinction of being chosen one of the first seven women magistrates of England. In March Mr. Ward had emergency surgery; she was suffering from bronchitis but visited him until she was unable to leave her bed. She died on March 24, 1920. So faithfully had she worked that one final novel, *Harvest,* appeared posthumously.

In her unfinished autobiography, *A Writer's Recollections* (1918), Mrs. Ward defends her right to use fiction to serve a cause; however, the majority of her works are dominated by her interest in what she considered the traditional and appropriate concern of women with matters of the heart and the divided concern of men with matters of the heart and matters of vocation or position. The following analysis of her work will be organized thematically rather than chronologically: her religious novels; her social reform novels; the "romances"; the reporting, novels, and autobiography of the war years, and a concluding evaluation.

CHAPTER 2

The Religious Works

MRS. Ward's meteoric rise to literary fame was due in large part to her successful portrayal of religious issues that had been troubling thousands in England, Europe, and America for much of the nineteenth century. For her sympathetic dramatization of orthodox belief and intellectual doubt she was prepared not only by her father's spiritual quest and the attendant changes in the family's fortunes, but also by her own studies and friendships with unorthodox Oxford scholars like Mark Pattison, Thomas Hill Green, Benjamin Jowett, and her uncle Matthew Arnold. Early in the century English rationalism had been strengthened by the works of the philosopher Immanuel Kant (1724–1804): *Critique of Pure Reason,* which appeared in 1781, and the more radical *Religion within the Bounds of Mere Reason,* which appeared in 1793 and brought him official censure. A subtler influence to rebellion came from the two poet-dramatists Johann Wolfgang von Goethe (1749–1832) and Johann Christoph Friedrich von Schiller (1759–1805), and the novelist Jean Paul Friedrich Richter (1763–1825), all favorites of Thomas Carlyle. Further attack on institutional orthodoxy came from Friedrich Daniel Ernst Schleiermacher's argument for the particularity of the individual, while Barthold Georg Niebuhr's three-volume *Roman History* (English translation 1828–42) established the method of source criticism that was to destroy the traditional authorships of Scripture. Schleiermacher (1768–1834) and Niebuhr (1776–1831) were introduced by the translations and comments of Bishop Thirwall.

However, one of the foremost champions of religious liberalism was Georg Wilhelm Friedrich Hegel (1770–1831), German philosopher sponsored in England by Benjamin Jowett and Arthur Stanley, both friends of the Arnold family. Central to Hegel's philosophical system was the conviction that while God is absolute truth, in religion this truth is veiled in imagery; furthermore, truth is the absence of error, but it is known to be truth only because error has been experienced and overcome by truth. But the argument most significant to Mrs. Ward's religious philosophy, as revealed not only in *Robert Elsmere* but in most of her works, comes from Hegel's *The Phenomenology of Mind* (1807), which brilliantly builds the theory of progressive racial enlightenment; that is, the human mind has risen from mere consciousness, through self-consciousness, reason, spirit, and religion, to absolute knowledge. Through Squire Wendover, the antagonist of *Robert Elsmere,* Mrs. Ward argues the challenge of this German scholarship—that the nineteenth-century mind so far exceeds the first-century mind that the Gospel narratives must be read as the fanciful creations of an age predisposed to miracles. Through Elsmere's response—suffering at the break with loved ones and familiar rituals but exhilaration at a new intellectual freedom—Mrs. Ward seems to be portraying her own remarkable spiritual and intellectual development in her study and friendships in Oxford, although she acknowledged only the influence of her uncle Matthew Arnold, whose *St. Paul and Protestantism* (1870), *Literature and Dogma* (1873), and *God and the Bible* (1875) advocate stripping Christianity of its miraculous elements.

I *Amiel's* Journal Intime, *1885*

Mrs. Ward's first major religious work, her translation of *The Journal Intime of Henri Frederic Amiel,* begun in 1884 and published in 1885, served to strengthen her belief in the individuality of religious experience and gave her insights into her father's spiritual quest as well as material for a number of characters in her novels. She began the work with the approval of the *Journal*'s French editor, M. Edmond Scherer, whom she had known for many years. The work was interrupted by the writing of her novel *Miss Bretherton* (1884) and before its appearance in December 1885 she was already full of plans for *Robert Elsmere.* Her work remains the standard English form of this great Swiss mystic's contribution to the literature of the inner life.

Henri Frederic Amiel was born in Geneva in September 1821, at the height of the city's prosperity under the French Republic.

However, in 1833—just as Geneva was beginning its decline—Amiel, at the age of twelve, lost both of his parents. This sensitive, impressionable, physically delicate boy, who was already disposed to a more or less melancholy and dreamy view of life, showed a deep interest in the religious problems and ideas that had characterized Geneva since the days of Calvin. Perhaps this meditative interest in his native city's habit of theological debate is the reason his university years were not outstanding, for the following period, from 1842–48, as he traveled and studied in Germany, Scandinavia, Holland, Austria, France, and England, proved to be a time of happiness and intellectual expansion. In 1848 his first mature writing appeared in *Bibliothèque Universelle;* but eight years later his reflective faculty had defeated his will to write for print. While his lectures remained carefully prepared, but dry as dust—for fear of seeming to use emotion to persuade rather than intellect to inform—he began his journal, which was to run to seventeen thousand folio pages.

Of Amiel Mrs. Ward says, in her introduction: "Both as poet and as psychologist, Amiel makes another link in a special tradition; he adds another name to the list of those who have won a hearing from their fellows as interpreters of the inner life, as the revealers of man to himself. He is the successor of St. Augustine and Dante. . . . What others have done for the spiritual life of other generations he has done for the spiritual life of this . . . ."[1] She points out his central distinction between religion and philosophy: "Religion, Amiel declares again and again, cannot be replaced by philosophy. The redemption of the intelligence is not the redemption of the heart. The philosopher and critic may succeed in demonstrating that the various definite forms into which the religious thought of man had thrown itself throughout history are not absolute truth, but only the temporary creations of a need which gradually and surely outgrows them all."[2] Then she quotes Amiel's challenge to philosophy: "The Trinity, the life to come, paradise and hell, may cease to be dogmas and spiritual realities, the form and the letter may vanish away—the question of humanity remains: What is it which saves?"[3] His answer to this question she finds very close to the one of Professor Thomas Hill Green and her own convictions: man is saved by the realization that "consciousness. . .as it has been painfully elaborated by human history, [is] the only revelation of God."[4]

The spiritual longings of Amiel and Thomas Arnold won Mrs. Ward's complete sympathy, so that despite her own rejection of authoritarian doctrine and revealed religion, she could write perceptively of the ritualist and the zealot as well as the humanist and the agnostic. Like her grandfather, Dr. Thomas Arnold, she felt the English Church should make room for everyone who wished to claim its fellowship; like her uncle, Matthew Arnold, who despite his assertion of loss of faith in the famous poem "Dover Beach" attended the Anglican Church with considerable regularity throughout his life, Mrs. Ward sought to change her nation's church to suit the nation's changing culture. This she hoped to accomplish through fiction. She wrote four "religious" novels: *Robert Elsmere* (1888) and its sequel, *The Case of Richard Meynell* (1911), both about the Established Church; *The History of David Grieve* (1892), the story of a self-taught intellectual humanist; and *Helbeck of Bannisdale* (1898), the powerful and tragic story of love between a devout Catholic and a strong-willed nonbeliever. However, few of her novels ignore the effect of religious practices, ranging from the brooding harshness of Isaac Costrell's ignorant Evangelicalism in *The Story of Bessie Costrell* (1895) to Eleanor's reconciliation to the crucifix, symbol of her early Catholic training, in *Eleanor* (1900), to Janet Leighton's saintly Quakerism in *Harvest* (1920).

II Robert Elsmere, *1888*

As early as 1871, Mary Arnold wrote to her future husband: "Traditional and conventional Christianity is worked out—certainly as far as the great artisan and intelligent working class of England is concerned, and all those who are young and touched, ever so vaguely and uncertainly, with the thought-atmosphere of the day. Is there a substitute which shall still be Christianity?"[5] Such a substitute was the basic concept of *Robert Elsmere,* whose hero finds liberation from the old faith and becomes the founder of the new faith for which the spiritually hungry public longed. That there was such a hunger seems confirmed by the book's remarkable sales record. In March, less than a month after its debut, the first edition of five hundred copies was exhausted and a second appeared. The third edition appeared April nineteenth and was sold in a week; it was followed shortly by a fourth edition.

When Gladstone's article in the May *Nineteenth Century* gave sales a new impetus, two more three-volume editions were sold during May, and a seventh, the last of the three-volume format, sold out in June. At the end of July a six-shilling edition of five thousand copies appeared; and one of seven thousand, in August, continued the sensational success of the novel. By January 1890, forty-four thousand copies of the six-shilling editions had been sold. A new half-crown edition reached the twenty thousand mark by November 1890; another twenty-three thousand copies were sold by the end of 1891. In retrospect, it is ironic that Macmillan, who had published her *Miss Bretherton* and Mr. Ward's *English Poets*, should have rejected the first few chapters of *Robert Elsmere* as a work not likely to interest the British public. Similar "best seller" records were set by the novel in America, although most were pirated editions. The book was also translated into most European languages, reflecting the religious turmoils occurring at different paces in each country.

Briefly, the story of *Robert Elsmere* is that of a young Oxford student, not brilliant but competent, more emotional than critical, who climaxes his university career by choosing to accept the Surrey clerical post offered by a relative. Before beginning his labors, he visits in the Westmoreland country, and there falls in love with Catherine Leyburn, the saintly head of her family of two sisters and a widowed mother. Catherine finally yields to her love for Robert, and the two begin an idyllic life of service to Robert's parish. But his continuing study, with the aid of the Squire's excellent library at Murewell Hall, and the stimulus of the disquieting questions asked by Edward Langham, Professor Grey, and Squire Wendover, lead Robert to the catastrophic admission that he can no longer honestly conduct the services of the Anglican Church. Catherine, a poorly educated evangelical, is heartbroken at her husband's apostasy and struggles for months to reach an uneasy compromise between her love for her husband and her own unshaken orthodox faith.

Robert gives up his church and moves his family to the East End of London in order to work out a New Brotherhood, which proves thrillingly successful in its appeal to the artisans of the area. He soon becomes a hero to both the workers and the intellectuals; and he dies a hero's death from overwork in the cause of the new faith. Catherine struggles valiantly with the dual role of loving wife and unhappy spectator at the "services" of the new religion. After Robert's death she continues her lifelong pattern of service to those in need, attends her own church, and cares for their infant daughter. A subplot, in which Rose, Catherine's talented, temperamental, rebellious youngest sister, is courted by both the melancholy Edward Langham and the charming Lord Flaxman, provides much of the interest of this three-volume novel.

The conflict develops when Squire Wendover hammers away at Robert's theological position by demanding that religious documents be subjected to the same critical evaluation that was applied to other historical material. He insists that man's power of apprehending and recording has vastly improved through the ages, that "the reasoning powers of the cave dweller have developed into the reasoning powers of a Kant,"[6] and that such reasoning powers cannot be shut out of religion. Even the gentle, compassionate Henry Grey tells Robert: "God is forever reason: and His communication, His revelation, is reason!"[7] As Robert's battle between emotion and reason, between orthodox faith and enlightened intellect reaches its climax, he asks:

> "*Do I believe in God?* Surely, surely! 'Though He slay me yet will I trust in Him!' *Do I believe in Christ?* Yes—in the teacher, the martyr, the symbol to us Westerns of all things heavenly and abiding, the image and pledge of the invisible life of the spirit—with all my soul and all my mind!
>
> "*But in the Man-God,* the Word from Eternity,—in a wonder-working Christ, in a risen and ascended Jesus, in the living Intercessor and Mediator for the lives of His doomed brethren?"[8]

His answer to this last question—every human soul that responds to the will of God shares equally with Jesus of Nazareth a divine sonship and that divine spark does not enable anyone, not even Jesus, to perform miracles—breaks his ties with traditional Trinitarian Christianity which asserts that Jesus was uniquely more than man and that the Holy Spirit can and does perform miracles.

Despite the fervor with which Mrs. Ward promoted this Unitarian interpretation of Christian dogma, she did not lose sight of the romance of human hearts living through these intellectual-spiritual pilgrimages. "Robert stood gazing at the home consecrated by love, by effort, by faith. The high alternations of intellectual and spiritual debate, the strange emerging sense of deliverance, gave way to a most bitter human pang of misery. 'Oh God! My wife—my work!' "[9] With keen insight into the psychological motivation of her characters, she communicates their inner drama: "Robert, man-like, in spite of all the griefs and sorenesses of the position, had immeasurably the best of it. In the first place such incessant activity of the mind as his is in itself both tonic and narcotic. It was constantly generating in him fresh purposes and hopes, constantly deadening regret, and pushing the old things out of sight."[10] Whereas Catherine found that "in proportion as Robert and she became more divided, her dead father resumed a ghostly hold upon her. There were days when she went about rigid and silent, in reality living altogether in the past, among the gray farms, the crags, the stony ways of the mountains."[11] However, the author's sympathy for Catherine does not keep her from condemning her as one who dissociates moral judgment from religious dogma, and she is sure that the saintly unbeliever will become the spiritual leader of the future.

The religious controversy the novel argues so graciously stirred a wide spectrum of response. Gladstone's article "*Robert Elsmere* and the Battle of Belief"[12] and the author's reply, "The New Reformation, a Dialogue,"[13] are perhaps the best-known articles in the ensuing debate. Mrs. Ward's friend Dean Wace took her liberalism to task and was challenged by Thomas Huxley. To the steady stream of articles in most of the leading magazines of England and Scotland were added those in American and Canadian periodicals, while the sermons attacking or supporting this renovation of Christianity were countless. One quite typical article, conservative but gracious, appeared in the *Quarterly Review* of October 1888. The writer acknowledges that the success of the novel is evidence that the book has touched some general source of concern. He praises the skill and perception with which Mrs. Ward portrays the loving relationship of Catherine and Robert, the suffering their mental and spiritual struggles entail. He calls attention to the balance produced by the contrast between Catherine and her sister Rose. But he firmly repudiates her theological argument:

We refrain, in deference partly to Mrs. Ward's services in other departments of learning, partly to her earnestness and sincerity, and partly to her sex, from expressing the censure which would ordinarily be due to a writer who engaged in an attack upon the received Christian faith with so imperfect a knowledge of the present conditions of the controversy, and consequently with such inevitable misrepresentations. . . . The proper answer to *Robert Elsmere* would be an equally good novel, which instead of killing Robert Elsmere off conveniently at the moment when his theories were being put to the test of practice, and ending by the greatest piece of romance in the whole book—the statement that the brotherhood he founded still exists—would describe the inevitable breakdown of such arbitrary assumptions and conventions under the stress of common sense, common history and common life.[14]

The article continues for six more pages in strong refutation of Mrs. Ward's specific "heresies." Although the majority of those who wrote or preached about the novel found her position untenable, her readers enjoyed the story, or the vicarious statement of their own rebellion against the established order, and looked forward to her next novel.

It was the contention of many of her early reviewers that Mrs. Ward was a worthy successor of the earlier Victorian novelists, that she followed closely in the train of such writers as Mrs. Elizabeth Gaskell and George Eliot. An evaluation of some of her writing traits may serve as points of comparison. She begins *Robert Elsmere,* as she does many of her other books, with a long description of the outdoor setting. The critic of the *Quarterly Review* article found this descriptive passage too long to be gotten through on his first attempt, but he also commented: "The narrative is relieved and illustrated, moreover, by a rare sympathy with nature and remarkable capacity for natural description." Furthermore, he feels that "a very impressive correspondence is maintained throughout between the scenery and the action, and in this, as in many other points, Mrs. Ward exhibits high artistic power."[15] In self-analysis, Mrs. Ward tells in her *A Writer's Recollections* (1918) that from early childhood she had had a sensitivity to nature quite out of the ordinary and a love of the Westmoreland countryside akin to that of the Lake Poets.

Robert Elsmere's Catherine Leyburn, striding resolutely across her rugged but beautiful native domain on an errand of mercy, is as appropriately set as Cathy Earnshaw-Linton of Emily Brontë's *Wuthering Heights,* or Eustacia Vye of Thomas Hardy's *The Return of the Native,* for Catherine seems to have been molded almost as much by the landscape as by her father's theology. Upon her marriage to Robert, Catherine leaves this Wordsworthian setting for the heaths of Surrey, a somber wood that lies symbolically between Murewell Hall and the Vicarage, and her first acquaintance with absentee landlords, villainous agents, and neglected tenants. The final setting is London's East End, where the backgrounds range from salons to slums, but Mrs. Ward's descriptions are neither elaborate nor graphic, for here she is more the reformer than the poet, seeing people rather than the color of buildings. Nor are all her outdoor settings equally successful; though she thrilled to the French and Italian scenes that she studied and used for such novels as *Eleanor,* or part of *David Grieve,* the insight is that of a visitor, not a native, and in *The Story of Bessie Costrell,* the beauty of the introductory setting seems more than inappropriate to the introduction of John Bolderfield, an unperceptive elderly laborer.

In the portrayal of people, both those glimpsed in a single incident and those threading their way throughout the novel, Mrs. Ward achieves her greatest success. For many readers the character of Catherine Leyburn Elsmere was the most effective creation in the book, and they were delighted to meet her again in the story of Richard Meynell. Others, unfamiliar or unsympathetic with the personality of saints, found Catherine's rigidity unbelievable. And although Mrs. Ward apparently believed that a woman of even strong convictions can and should place her religion second to her love, as Lucy Foster does in *Eleanor,* she recognized that some individuals are meant to find their strongest allegiance in religion (or rejection of traditional religion), as do the hero and heroine of *Helbeck of Bannisdale,* and Edward Newbury of *The Coryston Family.*

As the author points out in the preface to the Westmoreland Edition of her works, she knew actual persons much like her character creations. Catherine is a composite of several of her kinswomen; Langham is an unmystical version of Amiel, "the hapless intellectual tortured by paralysis of the will."[16] The probing intellect of the Squire recalls Mark Pattison, only in its spiritual quest—not in his ungracious manner or his dereliction of moral responsibility for the conditions of his tenants. The saintly Henry Gray is that noble and persuasive master of philosophic thought Thomas Hill Green. She does not identify the sources of either Robert or Rose, but it is easy to see her own intellectual pilgrimage in Robert and her artistic, musical temperament in Rose. To forestall the charge that Robert loses his faith too easily, Mrs. Ward tells the reader that Robert as an undergraduate made the transition from philosophic idealism to orthodox revealed religion with unusual ease, and that most of his concern as a clergyman was to be morally rather than intellectually strong. Nevertheless, Clyde deL. Ryals, in his introduction to a 1967 edition of *Robert Elsmere,* like many other modern critics, finds the great defect of this and other thesis novels that the "human being is rendered in terms of the idea he stands for." Ryals argues the inconsistency of Elsmere's portrait in that he is meant to represent the thirst for knowledge that can found a new, intellectually honest faith, but he is in reality "born for religion, [and] does not possess the scientific temper: he is motivated not by the desire to know but by the ideal of religious feeling, which manifests itself in service to his fellow men. Robert could no more give up his ideal than Catherine could abandon her traditional beliefs."[17] And William S. Peterson considers the novel a record of the inner struggle Mrs. Ward had throughout her life between rationalism and mysticism.[18]

Perhaps Mrs. Ward's romantic interest betrays her intellectual interest in the eyes of the critic, although it apparently did not to the general public; furthermore, her human interest makes possible memorable minor characters; three in *Robert Elsmere*—Newcombe, the fanatically dedicated high-churchman; Wardlow, the Comtist; and Hugh Flaxman, the democratic aristocrat—are the first of a long procession of such charming personalities. And in refutation to the critics' accusation that Mrs. Ward lacked humor, this novel presents Rector Thornburgh and Mrs. Thornburgh, the first of many quietly but delightfully humorous characters. Here, also, is the strong strain of realism which controls Mrs. Ward's romantic viewpoint. Yvonne Ffrench in her excellent book on Mrs. Gaskell summarizes the frequent comparison of George Eliot and Mrs. Gaskell; "The one [Eliot] is powerful, the other [Gaskell] gentle; the one intellectual, the other emotional."[19] Mrs. Ward seems a synthesis of the two. Like Eliot she began with an idea, then clothed it with characters; but like Mrs. Gaskell, she was primarily concerned with what conflicting ideas do to people. Robert and Catherine are almost too good to be true, but Mrs. Ward does not perform a miracle to bridge the chasm between their religious experiences. And in the romance of Rose and Langham she wisely resists any sentimental temptation to have love make a "new man" of Langham. Yet she does not handle these fictitious persons with the aloofness of Eliot, nor with the cynical wit of Austen. One senses that the author had lived closely and affectionately with the Roses (much like her mother as well as herself) and the Catherines, with the Langhams (with traits like her father) and the Roberts and the Squires of real life.

There is a further similarity between Mrs. Gaskell's and Mrs. Ward's work that is striking. In Mrs. Gaskell's *North and South*, written thirty-three years before *Robert Elsmere*, three of the main characters are the Hales. Mr. Hale, after more than twenty years in his rustic parish, has studied himself out of faith with his earlier convictions and decides he can no longer be a minister of the Anglican Church. Near the beginning of the book he tells his eighteen-year-old daughter, Margaret, of his decision, but not of the process that brought him to it. She is deeply disturbed at his apostasy, but loves him dearly and prefers that he not try to explain himself. Mrs. Hale is utterly unable to cope with the situation. The family are forced to move to Milton, a mill town, and live in unattractive surroundings, while Mr. Hale augments their meager income by tutoring some ambitious mill bosses. He is assisted by the only friend in whom he can confide, a Cambridge professor. The Hales are less heroic than Robert and Catherine, but the poignancy of their ordeal attests to Mrs. Gaskell's knowledge as well as her talent. Elizabeth Gaskell was the daughter of a minister who left the ministry, and the wife of a Unitarian minister, in Manchester. One wonders if Mrs. Ward knew this or other Gaskell novels. Certainly her Marcella strongly resembles Margaret Hale, and the hero of *David Grieve* bears a strong likeness to the hero of *North and South*, Mr. Thornton, the mill manager who hungers for education and experiments with a cooperative kitchen for his workers. This is not to suggest that Mrs. Ward's characters are in any sense copies; rather, both women had experienced and observed social and human characteristics that fed both their artistic and moral needs.

The most serious criticism leveled against *Robert Elsmere* as a novel is that its purpose is too obvious. However, many Victorian novels were written to promote the author's philosophy or some worthy cause. Two of Mrs. Gaskell's novels, *Mary Barton* (1848) and *North and South* (1855), were written in the conviction that if the two sides of the labor-management struggle would but come to know each other, much of the violence and bitterness would disappear. Dickens's fascinating but distorted pictures of debtors' prison, Chancery, schools, and so on were not incidental to his popularity, nor are they unrelated to his lasting greatness. Charlotte Brontë's charity school in *Jane Eyre* was more than a retelling of her own unhappy experience in such a school, at Cowan Bridge, Lancaster: it was an effective protest against the ugly side of charity. Margaret Maison, in her *Studies in the Religious Novel,* reminds the critical reader that the novel, like most of the arts, found inspiration and nurture in religious agencies. She cites John Bunyan, frequently called the "father of the novel," and the legends of the Grail, as in Malory's *Morte D'Arthur,* but more pertinently demonstrates that the achievement of respectability and popularity as a literary genre was largely due to the Victorian discovery of the power of the religious novel.

> Religious novels of that time were not, as mid-twentieth-century readers might imagine, novels merely coloured by Christian thought and feeling, interpreting characters and events from a Christian standpoint; they bore a far more distinctive label than that. Nor were they just novels about clerical life, like those of Anthony Trollope (who from a spiritual point of view, did not penetrate very deep beneath the surplice). To the Victorian reader religious novels meant "theological romance"; Oxford Movement, novels of religious propaganda designed to disseminate a variety of forms of Christian belief, and assorted spiritual biographies in fiction including converts' confessions of all kinds, from the apologies of ardent agnostics to the testimonies of Catholic "perverts." . . . It was the Oxford Movement which really launched the religious novel on a large scale. This storm that rent the Establishment, sweeping some into safe harbour and casting others, wrecked and desolate, on every theological and philosophical shore, was responsible for a perfect *furor scribendi;* its lightnings fired the imagination of countless Victorians and from the eighteen-forties onwards we find young teenagers, middle-aged matrons, elderly governesses, statesmen, undergraduates and innumerable clerics of widely varying creeds, ages and talents all busily engaged in writing religious novels, chiefly for propaganda purposes.[20]

The roster of authors Margaret Maison discusses includes William Arnold (brother of Thomas and Matthew and uncle of Mrs. Ward), Robert Buchanan, Marie Corelli, Benjamin Disraeli, George De Maurier, George Eliot, Elizabeth Gaskell, Thomas Hardy, Nathaniel Hawthorne, Joseph Hocking, Charles Kingsley, John Henry Newman, Walter Pater, Mary Augusta Ward, Lew Wallace, William Hale White, and William Butler Yeats. So *Robert Elsmere* spoke *to* and *for* its time and followed in a worthy train. And while its specific religious issues are outdated, the dramatization of the role of religion in marriage and in the working out of a career has lasting relevance.

Furthermore, among the (sometimes more talented) voices descrying the period's decadence, Mrs. Ward offered *hope.* Sociologists explain the Victorian Age's optimism and complacency as the result of no serious warfare; the expansion of the Empire to its greatest limits; the absorption of the evolutionary theory that "survival of the fittest" justifies industrial and colonial expansion and assures mankind that he is on an escalator going "up." Mrs. Ward thrilled to the intellectual excitement of the adolescence of the age of science; she basked in the satisfaction of her own climb to eminence; she accepted without question the Victorian conviction that the ideal man is the educated English gentleman, member of the ruling class and sensitive and magnanimous in his relations with women. In each of these responses to life she was true to her times. J. Stuart Walters, writing on *Mrs. Humphry Ward, Her Work and Influence,* in 1912, says that "in the personality of Elsmere is struck the joyous note of hope and constructiveness that has been ringing quietly through the land since the dawn of the new century. Elsmere stands for a creed of no mere arid Unitarianism but for a Religion of Action—a blessed blend of all that is best in Christianity, with much that is good in the ideals of Marx and Spencer."[21] Her essential optimism is the highlight of her conversation with William Gladstone on the theme of *Robert Elsmere.* To his comment: "I believe in a degeneracy of man, in the Fall—in *sin*—in the intensity and virulence of sin. No other religion but Christianity meets the sense of sin, and sin is the great fact in the world to me," she replied that though she did not wish to deny the existence of moral evil, "the more one thought of it the more plain became its connection with physical and social and therefore *removable* conditions."[22] Later she summed it up in a letter to the great man: "Does not the difference between us on the question of sin come very much to this—that to you the great fact in the world and in the history of man is *sin*—to me, progress?"[23]

Modern criticism must conclude that Mrs. Ward's most famous novel is a good novel, well organized, artistically successful in many ways and worthy to represent its time. It is not a great novel, perhaps because its author was too close to her times, perhaps because it does several things well—none superbly; perhaps, like all of her novels, it is too carefully balanced between realism and romance, between intellect and emotion, between individualism and society. Nonetheless, as a number of recent editions of the novel attest, the drama of *Robert Elsmere* should seem peculiarly modern to a generation interested in Bishop John Robinson's *Honest to God* (1963), Harvey Cox's *The Secular City* (1965), and the intense debate between those committed to Progress and the disillusioned enemies of the Establishment. "If the hero's Christology is not the Christology of modern theologians, it nevertheless bears an amazing family likeness to Rudolf Bultmann's 'demythologized' Christ and to Dietrich Bonhoeffer's 'man for others'! Students of both literature and theology should be able to recognize the contemporaneity of *Robert Elsmere*."[24]

III The History of David Grieve, *1892*

Mrs. Ward's next novel, *The History of David Grieve,* presents her concept of a "new" Christianity from the point of view of the intelligent working class—outside both the university and the Established Church. David and Louie Grieve are living with their aunt and uncle, Hannah and Reuben Grieve, on a sheep farm in Derbyshire, across Kinder Scout from Manchester. David remembers his father and his dying charge to David to care for his sister, Louie. Their mother, a very pretty but selfish Frenchwoman, had deserted them, and later committed suicide. The children have an inheritance of £600, entrusted by their father to his former partner, Mr. Gurney; but their termagant aunt will not let their uncle tell them of it for fear they will leave and she will lose the £60 a year paid her by Mr. Gurney for their keep.

Mr. Ancrum, the crippled minister of the Clough End Chapel

they attend, takes a special interest in David, as do also 'Lisa Dawson, a former schoolteacher, and his wife, Margaret. These three encourage David's interest in books. David reads most of the time when he is not helping Reuben with the sheep. Louie, who hates to read but loves clothes and dramatizing herself, is utterly without normal affection; she hates Hannah, who hates her, and teases her brother even when he tries to be nice. After a temporary "conversion" experience and a struggle with the area bully, John Wigson, David runs away to Manchester, where he quickly learns the ways of the book business, outwits his bigoted employer, Purcell, tastes the delights of philosophical debating and the friendship and admiration of a wide assortment of people, including a Lord and Lady Driffield.

When David finally sends for Louie, Reuben tells them of the £600. They claim it and take a holiday in Paris, where David falls deeply in love with an independent young artist, and Louie runs away with another artist, a man of dissolute character. David and Elsie Delauney spend three almost perfect weeks of illicit love; then Elsie chooses her art rather than marriage, disappearing at the "command" of her art teacher. David hunts unsuccessfully for both Elsie and Louie; then he arranges that Louie and her lover, M. Mountjoie, shall have all that is left of the £600 if they will marry, while he tries to commit suicide. Mr. Ancrum finds him in time and nurses him back to health, to an acceptance of his loss of Elsie, and to a new interest in the spiritual claims of Christ.

Louie has a daughter, Cecile, in whose name she makes frequent demands for money from David. David marries Lucy Purcell, his former employer's pretty but shallow daughter. They have a son, Sandy; David becomes a successful bookseller and printer, but insists upon experimenting with cooperative profits, apprentice schools, and the like rather than spending his profits as Lucy would like, on social aggrandizement. Very slowly Lucy gains some maturity, then suddenly makes an incredible transformation as she is brought to an early death by sarcoma. Cecile dies of diphtheria and Louie disappears. Overwork forces David to return to Kinder Low for a rest; he rents a farm near Reuben and Hannah, a Hannah much mellowed by suffering and able to enjoy the captivating Sandy. One day David thinks he hears Louie calling him. He goes to Paris, where he finds her deserted by the young artist to whom she had become attached since Cecile's death. She agrees to return to England with him, but instead, commits suicide.

Through all these experiences, since David's arrival in Manchester, has moved Dora Lumox, cousin of Lucy, daughter of the owner of the Fruit and Flowers Parlour (a vegetarian restaurant and debating center), saintly high-churchwoman, expert needleworker. She is in love with David but maintains her sisterly manner faithfully, and he treats her much as he would the sister he wishes he had had. Dora's father is an undisciplined man who has several times deserted his wife and daughter and loses the Parlour as drink and another attack of wanderlust overcome him. Dora's natural seriousness has been strengthened by her father's instability and her mother's death, and after "Daddy" Lumox disappears, she lives with another single woman, becomes foreman of her needlework shop, and vicariously shares all David's adventures. In the epilogue David is content with his work, his son, his highly exalted memories of Lucy, his unorthodox faith, and his brotherly relationship to Dora, while Dora is awarded the doubtful blessing of her father's return, on Christmas Eve.

This novel has a Dickensian flavor. David has some of the charm of David Copperfield, and, of the two girls available, he chooses to marry the pretty, shallow one. "Daddy" Lumox is a sort of Mr. Micawber. Hannah and Reuben Grieve resemble Joe Gargery and Mrs. Joe of *Great Expectations.* The vindictive, self-righteous Purcell and his second wife, and the bullying John Wigson could be matched with several Dickens characters. The "typical" Ward religious figure, a combination of Amiel, T. H. Green, and her own father, is the saintly Ancrum. And the romantic challenge is briefly but effectively portrayed in Regnault, an artist who is adored by the "rats" of Bohemian Paris, who honors David with interest and sincere advice, and who later dies in the war with Germany. Perhaps because all of the characters in this novel are more the creation of her imagination than a recreation of people familiar to her, Mrs. Ward invests more passion in all the novel's conflicts and draws her characters in bolder colors. Louie's strangeness is well handled, with a consistency that is realistic and frustrating. David's extrasensory hearing of Louie's call reminds one of Jane Eyre's similar telepathic response to Mr. Rochester's need. Lucy's death scene is sentimentally Victorian and is quite obviously used as a vehicle for Mrs. Ward's contention that spiritual experience is individual and dependent upon the heightened sensitivity of suffering.

The religious theme, played over a wider range than in *Robert Elsmere,* includes Ancrum, the saintly doubter; Dora, the saintly High-Church communicant; Louie, a worldly Catholic; Purcell, the bigoted dissenter; Dyson, the ignorant evangelist; Lucy's humble, pious relatives; and David, self-educated humanist. Of Dyson, Mrs. Ward says: "He was slow and pompous; his tone with the Almighty might easily have roused a hostile sense of humour; but Dissent in its active and emotional forms kills the sense of humour; and besides—there was real, ungainly power in the man. Every phrase of his opening prayer was hackneyed; every gesture uncouth. But his heart was in it, and religious conviction is the most infectious thing in the world."[25]

The description of Ancrum is the fullest and the most touching. After a visit with David, who is so sure of his own capacities and his own intellectual convictions, the minister asks himself: "Is there any 'soul,' any 'personality' for the man who is afflicted and weakened with intermittent melancholia? Where is his identity, where his responsibility? And if there is none for him, how does the accident of health bestow them on his neighbor?"[26] His brooding intellect feeds on the writings of Huxley, and Newman, books of mental pathology and High-Church manuals of self-examination. Ancrum had had his moment of significance when he felt called to preach. But after a few years of congenial, humble service, his health and his spirit had broken. He had also had his moment of romance—marriage to a girl of some beauty but of an undeveloped, sensuous nature that could not long endure the rarified life of service. His broken heart he had buried in arduous service in the cotton famine. After the shattering experience at Clough End Chapel, he spent his small strength teaching and befriending neglected boys in the mills of Manchester. In the end he joins the Catholic Church, hoping there to end his spiritual uncertainties.

David's religious experience includes a "conversion" under the praying and preaching of Dyson, the inevitable "falling from grace" in this limited dogma, the exciting discovery of Secularism (the popular form of Positivism), the philosophical implications of Science, and finally a "Christianity" that was positive, fruitful, and human. David speaks for the author:

In the old days . . . I was constantly troubled and not for myself only, but for others, the poor and unlearned especially, who, as it seemed to me, would lose most in the crumbling of the Christian mythology—as to the intellectual difficulties of the approach to God. All this philosophical travail of two thousand years—and so many doubts and darknesses! A world athirst for preaching, and nothing simple or clear to preach—when once the miracle-child of Bethlehem had been dispossessed. And *now* it is daylight-plain to me that in the simplest act of loving self-surrender there is the germ of all faith, the essence of all lasting religion. Quicken human service, purify and strengthen human love, and have no fear but that the conscience will find God! For all the time this quickening and this purification are His work in thee.[27]

The sermonette continues through the usual condemnation of "dogmatic overlay" and "wonder-loving additions" to the assurance that "the actual voice, the first meaning" can be recovered in this simple doctrine of brotherly love, as authentic in Greek philosophy as in the modern expressions of humanism.

Once again the quarterlies raged against Mrs. Ward's theology and were uncertain of her artistry. In the preface to the 1892 edition she defends herself against their contradictory comments: "tiresome as a novel and ineffectual as a sermon"; "a powerful story, at times of absorbing interest"; "total absence of humour"; "a refined and delicate sense of humour"; "distinctly and surprisingly inferior to its predecessor"; "has greater interest, more passion, more power, and more pathos."[28] She confounds them with their dictums—an author can write sincerely only of his own experience, but if he is too autobiographical, he is unimaginative. And she calls to the witness stand a long list of great novels and novelists to prove her literary right to write a novel burdened with religious and philosophical matter.

Without doubt the novel has a freshness and an imaginativeness unique among her novels. Its tone is somber, achieving pathos rather than humor in Lucy's debacle at the Driffields', Daddy Lumox's denunciation of his brother-in-law, and similar scenes. David's passionate attachment to Elsie and his dispassionate attachment to Lucy show remarkable insight and daring frankness for that day. Some of her characters are described too fully, perhaps because, like Lucy, they do not really come alive; but others are hauntingly convincing; for example, Louie. It is interesting that in *Eleanor,* Mrs. Ward's most Jamesian novel, there is again an "insane" sister for the hero, briefly but effectively drawn. The religious message is handled with care in the delineation of characters to fit the varieties of religious experience; but David's convictions are typical of intellectuals who have never known the Church or its teachings at their best, and therefore carry conviction only to David's class ("enlightened" or partially educated working men), not to Mrs. Ward's university-trained peers.

IV Helbeck of Bannisdale, *1898*

The story of Mrs. Ward's third religious novel, *Helbeck of Bannisdale*, begins as Alan Helbeck waits to receive his widowed sister and her stepdaughter, during Lent. The season is very important to this devoutly Catholic household. Laura Fountain—small, lovely, quick, intelligent, and musical—even as a child was a strangely independent, gay person, hardly seeming to miss the real mother who had died in Laura's infancy. She had become learned without disciplined study, in close association with her father, a Cambridge professor who rejected all "revealed" religion. He had come from a farm near Bannisdale, glad to have escaped the farming way of life still carried on by his relatives, the Masons. Laura finds the countryside speaks to her of kinship, and she sincerely tries to find good in her cousins, fanatically Protestant Elizabeth Mason; buxom, wholesome Polly; and handsome, musical, but crude Hubert. Thirteen years before, when Laura was eight, she and her father had visited the Masons, then gone to a second-rate watering place, Potter's Beach, where they had met Augustina Helbeck. To the lonely professor, Augustina had poured out her unhappiness under the austerity imposed upon Bannisdale by her brother, twelve years her junior. Stephen Fountain offered her escape and the courage to defy her brother: he enjoyed leading her away from the faith she obviously did not understand. But when Stephen died, she was frightened into a return to her earlier faith and desired to return to Bannisdale.

Laura, always the more mature personality, loyally comes with her convalescent stepmother and tries to understand the faith of those about her. She insists upon the right to visit her relatives and even to share their social life, until Hubert disgraces her by publicly laying claim to her interest. Later she goes with Polly to the city of Froswick, to visit Hubert. Again the "date" ends badly, and Laura walks eight miles home, to be carried, exhausted, the last few yards, in the arms of Alan Helbeck. The two can no longer deny their attraction for each other, and the first hours of sweet surrender are all that could be desired. But almost immediately Alan's faith begins to impose itself. He thinks of the glorification of their love that her conversion will bring; on the other hand, his counsellors and servants fear the change that marriage and possible heirs will make in the dedication of Bannisdale's resources to Catholic charities. Laura tries, but finds the authoritarianism of the Church, and the invasion of her privacy demanded by the total dedication Alan practices, more than she can stand. She flees to friends at Cambridge, the Friedlands. She is called back for Augustina's sake. Her stepmother dies. Laura once again surrenders to the fineness of Alan and the love that exists between them. But she discovers that the very will she depended upon to make her a good wife will not let her surrender herself to the way of life that must come first for Alan. She drowns herself, and Alan turns to the Jesuit vocation he had contemplated before they met.

Helbeck of Bannisdale, though it deals once again with the clash of beliefs, was conceived as a tragedy, and is unquestionably Mrs. Ward's best novel. It sold less than her previous novels, but it deserves the discriminating praise it received. George Meredith wrote, "I know not another book that shows the classic fate so distinctly. . . ." And Lord Crewe said, "The hero, if hero he be, is as fresh a creation as Ravenswood or Rochester . . . and though the atmosphere is so much less lurid and troubled, I have something of the *Wuthering Heights* sense of coming disaster."[29] And European critics, such as Carlo Segre, a competent Italian student of English literature, found *Helbeck* one of the finest English novels of its own five-year period.[30]

Helbeck had two sources—Thomas Arnold's history and Mrs. Ward's visit, in the autumn of 1896, with her friends Mr. James Cropper and his daughter, in the beautiful South Westmoreland country. One day the talk was concerned with the fortunes of an old Catholic family, the Stricklands, who had owned Sizergh Castle, near Sedgwick, for more than three centuries, enduring persecutions but falling beneath a modern weight of poverty and mortgages. By the end of her return journey to London, the next day, Mrs. Ward had thought out her story. But all through the ensuing winter she steeped herself in Catholic literature. Added to her usual careful preparation for all her writing was awareness of her personal involvement in such a conflict, through her mother and father's experience, and a deepening conviction that there was more than one way that a man might seek salvation. In the spring, through the good offices of Mr. Cropper, the Ward family were able to live for some months in Levens Hall, a wonderful old Tudor house near the mouth of the Kent. Unlike Bannisdale, Levens was well cared for, but it had a ghostly "gray lady," of sadly modern origin, whom Mrs. Ward wove into her story; and the estate was the center for the fell farms, the mournful peat-bog, the daffodils, and the Fell Chapel which appear in the story.

Through the ruined splendor of Bannisdale—gradually being stripped of its last treasures to serve charitable enterprises—and the uneven beauty of the little chapel move a small but choice collection of minor characters: the gentle but eccentric Father Bowles, the nun with a face "at once sweet and peevish," the hostile Father Leadham, converted Cambridge professor, the orphan children, and the young nun whose harsh mechanical participation in ritual suddenly becomes the sweet song of true worship. To an ex-Catholic friend, Mr. Addis, who was reading her manuscript, Mrs. Ward wrote concerning the two main characters:

> In my root-idea of him, Helbeck was to represent the old Catholic crossed with that more mystical and enthusiastic spirit, brought in by such converts as Ward and Faber, under Roman and Italian influence. I gather, both from books and experience, that the more fervent ideas and practices, which the old Catholics of the 'forties disliked, have, as a matter of fact, obtained a large ascendency in the present practice of Catholics, just as Ritualism has forced the hands of the older High Churchmen. And I thought one might in the matter of austerities, conceive a man directly influenced by the daily reading of the Lives of the Saints, and obtaining in middle life, after probation and under special circumstances, as it were, leave to follow his inclinations.
>
> I take note most gratefully of all your small corrections. What I am really anxious about now is the points—in addition to pure jealous misery—on which Laura's final breach with Helbeck would turn. I *think* on the terror of confession—on what would seem to her the inevitable uncovering of the inner life and yielding of personality that the Catholic system involves—and on the foreignness of the whole idea of *sin*, with its relative, penance.[31]

Mrs. Ward also sought the approval of her project from Lord Acton, a renowned English Catholic, and from her father. With the latter she discussed her growing recognition of the intellectual preeminence of Newman, and her horror at the misuse of the body often sanctioned in the lives of the saints.

That Mrs. Ward continued to find much in Catholicism that was of interest to her is clear by her sympathetic use of this faith in her later novels, especially *Eleanor.* But the characteristically balanced fairness of her presentation and the remarkable welding of faith to character make *Helbeck* a modern Greek tragedy. The eternal force of the struggle between Alan and Laura is well expressed through some of the comments made by Dr. Friedland. He explains to his wife that Laura could have resisted a fetish-filled, unreasonable form of Catholicism, but all that is romantically imaginative in her is captured by Helbeck's form of the faith: the best of English qualities disciplined by heroic memories of persecution and hardship. Yet her father's temperament and training force her to maintain her self-respect and examine "the claims of this great visible system. Her reason refuses them—but why? She cannot tell. For Heaven's sake, why do we leave our children's minds empty" of the education they need to resolve their doubts.[32] And to a fellow professor Friedland comments:

"The Catholic war with history is perennial! History, in fact, is the great rationalist; and the Catholic conscience is scandalized by her. And so we have these pitiful little books—" he laid his hand on the volume beside him—"which simply expunge history, or make it afresh. And we have a piece of Jesuit *apologia,* like this paper of Leadham's—so charming, in a sense, so scholarly! And yet one feels through it a cry of the soul—the Catholic arraignment of history. . . ."[33]

He continues, arguing that England was lost to the Church not by the villainy of a Tudor king or his bishops but by the revolt of the common intelligence, the common conscience. He concedes the symbolic appeal of the Church, but chooses a greater symbol:

". . . The figure of the Church,—spouse or captive, bride or martyr,—as she has become personified in Catholic imagination, is surely among the greatest, the most ravishing, of human conceptions. It ranks with the image of 'Jahve's Servant' in the poetry of Israel. And yet behind her, as she moves through history, the modern sees the rising of something more majestic still—the free human spirit, in its contact with the infinite sources of things!"[34]

Alan Helbeck is the product of the Catholic concept of history; Laura Fountain the product of the "modern" concept of history. They are unusual personalities, both superior to the common masses upon which religious and philosophical concepts seek to place their rule. The web of circumstances which imprisons them is designed by either an all-wise God misinterpreted by fallible human beings, or by the impersonal, inexorable forces of the upward evolving history of man. Yet, in true tragic form, each makes his own decision, each chooses a loyalty more demanding than the usually all-powerful idol of human love.

Thus Laura becomes a modern Antigone, dying in defense of the individual's right to battle institutional authority. The outstanding achievement of the author is that Laura rises to meet her heroic decision from immaturity to a self-knowledge greater than that of any other character in the story. Her last note—a cry of mind, heart, and soul—unites the affectionate stepdaughter, the loyal daughter, the woman deeply in love, and the heroic individual:

"But when they left me with her [her dying step-mother], I seemed to be holding not her hand, but his [her father's]. I was back in the old life—I heard him speaking quite distinctly. 'Laura, you cannot do it, *you cannot do it*!' And he looked at me in sorrow and displeasure. I argued with him so long, but he beat me down. And the voice I seemed to hear was not his only,—it was the voice of my own life, only far stronger and crueller than I have ever known it.

"Cruel!—I hardly know what I am writing—who has been cruel! I!—only I! To open the old wounds—to make him [Alan Helbeck] glad for an hour—then to strike and leave him—could anything be more pitiless? Oh! my best beloved. . . . But to live a lie—upon his heart, in his arms—that would be worse. I don't know what drives me exactly—but the priests want my inmost will—want all that is I—and I know when I sit down to think quietly, that I cannot give it. I knew it last October. But to be with him, to see him, was too much. Oh! if God hears, may He forgive me—I prayed to-night that He would give me courage."[35]

One is moved to ask, as after a study of Sophocles's *Antigone*, whose tragedy is the greater, that of the young woman who dies convinced of the necessity of her action, or the man who goes on living with his failure to understand the real conflict between them. Mrs. Ward has succeeded in creating a novel from which no character, portion of the setting, or turn of the plot can wisely be eliminated. Furthermore, the conflict—whether defined as the old versus the new, the institution versus the individual, faith versus doubt, submission versus willfulness, or history versus heroism—is eternal. This novel of Mrs. Ward's should be rediscovered by future reading generations.

V The Case of Richard Meynell, *1911*

The last of her religious novels, *The Case of Richard Meynell,* can only seem an anticlimax to the preceding works, yet it is never bad or completely inconsequential. Catherine Elsmere reappears, to the delight of her admirers, and suffers the second ordeal of her saintly life when her daughter falls in love with a man who, like Robert, finds he must abandon the orthodox faith. Hugh and Rose Flaxman have taken temporary residence at Upcote Minor and insist that Catherine and her twenty-six-year-old-daughter, Mary, come to a cottage nearby, for Catherine's health. Richard Meynell, the mature, dedicated, bachelor rector, who has served Upcote for twenty years, has been charged with heresy and knows that the Modernist movement, so much stronger than in the days of Robert Elsmere, is to meet a test of its strength in his trial. There are an assortment of characters who complicate Meynell's life, but the mysteries are explained, the guilty identified, and Catherine has a "vision" of Robert that assures her Mary will be happy in her union with Meynell. Mrs. Ward again argues her own position in a death-bed scene, but she reveals in Meynell's answers to the dying workman's questions a rather inarticulate spokesman for his church party. His sermon at the trial is good preaching but poor theology, and his side loses, although convinced that they have made progress in liberalizing the Church. Hester, Meynell's ward, and an illegitimate niece in the proper but dull Fox-Whilton family, is an unconvincing rebel; and the failure of Meynell's influence on his ward is a strangely contradictory argument for an author who insists that the only power of religion or God in the affairs of men is human influence.

Once again the author indulges in too much scenery, although no single passage is long. The novel cries out for more "inner scenery"—less English weather and countryside. Canon Dornal and his playful kitten are delightful, though this one gleam of humor is hardly adequate for a whole novel. With her usual fairness, the author makes the bishop and the canon who oppose Meynell completely lovable, and excuses their mistaken position on the grounds of the necessity of defense of their institution. Squire Barron is a pathetic villain; his scheming is melodramatic but true to the segment of the church and society that he represents, a segment that clothes personal frustrations and ambitions in the sacred vestures of the warriors of faith. Meynell is a more masculine hero than Robert Elsmere, but is still too saintly.

In this presentation of her faith, twenty-two years after *Robert Elsmere* and after the disappointing results of her own attempt at a cultural religion offered at the Passmore Edwards Settlement House, the author no longer proposes a New Brotherhood, but a simplified worship service and a human Christ. She feels sure that the Christ who mistakenly called himself divine has become by some

"mysterious and unique destiny . . . Spirit and Idea. . . . Many men, in all ages and civilizations have dreamed of a City of God, a Kingdom of Righteousness, an Ideal State, and a Divine Ruler. Jesus alone has made of that dream, history; has forced it upon, and stamped it into history. The Messianic dream of Judaism—though wrought of nobler tissue—is not unlike similar dreams in other religions; but in this it is unique, that it gave Jesus of Nazareth his opportunity, and that from it has sprung the Christian Church. Jesus accepted it with the heart of a child; he lived in it; he died for it; and by means of it, his spiritual genius, his faithfulness unto death transformed a world. He died indeed, overwhelmed; with the pathetic cry of utter defeat upon his lips. And the leading races of mankind have knelt ever since to the mighty spirit who dared not only to conceive and found the Kingdom of God, but to think of himself as its Spiritual King—by sheer divine right of service, of suffering, and of death! . . ."[36]

The confused eloquence of this sermon clearly exemplifies the limitation of the religious novel, even in the capable hands of Mrs. Ward. And so perhaps her critics were correct in challenging her right to supply the untrained minds of the laity with high-sounding but ill-defined theological terms clothed in the emotional appeal of a good story, rather than the straightforward presentation of dogma to be found in nonfiction studies of the subject. But the religious freedom that would permit high and low, conservative and liberal believers full citizenship within the national church is a cause most modern readers could support. In the Foreword to the novel Mrs. Ward makes a direct appeal for this support from her American readers.

May I ask those of my American readers who are not intimately acquainted with the conditions of English rural and religious life to remember that the dominant factor in it—the factor on which the story of Richard Meynell depends—is the existence of the State Church, of the great ecclesiastical corporation, the direct heir of the pre-Reformation Church, which owns the cathedrals and the parish churches, which by right of law speaks for the nation on all national occasions, which crowns and marries and buries the Kings of England, and, through her bishops in the House of Lords, exercises a constant and important influence on the law-making of the country? This Church possesses half the elementary schools, and is the legal religion of the great public schools which shape the ruling upper class. She is surrounded with the prestige of centuries, and it is probable that in many directions she was never so active or so well served by her members as she is at present.[37]

It is the struggle to weaken the heritage and influence of this great institution—by the nonconformists, by the nonbelievers, and even by the feuding Anglicans—that Mrs. Ward deplores and seeks to dramatize in the lives of individuals in the hope that new tolerance and a more intellectually acceptable theology will revitalize the Church's ameliorating influence on men and nations. Her interest in religion appears again and again in the rest of her books, but the emphasis shifts to social reform, to romance, to the great national experience of war. Although her dream of a "new Christianity" has not materialized, and few modern readers are interested in her battles of faith, she clearly wrote of and for her times, with sincerity and skill.

CHAPTER 3

The Social Reform Novels

MRS. Ward's conviction that moral evil is due chiefly to bad physical and social—therefore remediable—conditions led to both challenging novels and hard-earned reforms. In the role of reformer she began, as she did her writing apprenticeship, in Oxford, where she became, in the winter of 1873-74, the secretary and one of the moving spirits of a committee organized to secure more adequate education for women. This effort culminated in the founding of Somerville Hall, a residence for women, in 1878. This work was excellent training for the more sustained effort required to establish Passmore Edwards Settlement, in London, a project intended to prove the efficacy of the "New Brotherhood" sketched in *Robert Elsmere*. The plans for the settlement were begun in 1890, and the facilities were opened in 1897. However, Mrs. Ward's support and leadership continued for many years, as the emphasis shifted from "enlightening" religion and cultural refinement, to Children's Play Schools, Vacation Schools, and Crippled Children's School. Her justified prominence as a humanitarian was largely responsible for such honors as being chosen, in January 1920, as one of the first woman magistrates of England, an honorary position which entitled her to an escort of police at her funeral; and the honorary LL.D. degree bestowed upon her in March 1920 by the University of Edinburgh. The settlement still serves its community—under the name of Mary Ward House.

The five novels that reflect her interest in reform are *Marcella*, 1894; *Bessie Costrell*, 1895; *Sir George Tressady*, 1896; *Daphne*, or *Marriage à la Mode*, 1909; and *Delia Blanchflower*, 1915. The third book is a sequel to the first, and therefore will follow it in this study, although *Marcella* deals primarily with the evils of the game laws and *George Tressady* is concerned with a Factory Bill and the problems of miners. The short novel *Bessie Costrell* is really just a long short story, based, as are many of her plots, on a true incident, but pleading the case of the "sinful" lower class without recommending any "remedy." *Daphne,* the poorest of her novels, makes an attack upon the American divorce laws because they seemed to her to sabotage English traditions. *Delia Blanchflower* deals with the woman's suffrage movement, of which she disapproved even more than she did the American divorce laws, but about which she wrote a better novel.

I Marcella, *1894*

Marcella, the last of her two-volume works (many Victorian novels were two or three volumes, too long for changing public taste; *Robert Elsmere*'s original format was three volumes), is the best of her "reform" novels. An early review of the novel said: "Quite as truly as *Robert Elsmere, Marcella* is a story of immediately contemporaneous life and thought. It is more readable, considered as a story, than *Robert Elsmere* or *David Grieve.* As a vehicle for the discussion of current social problems, it is by far more lucid and more satisfactory than either of its predecessors."[1] The heroine of the first volume of the novel is, like Rose in *Robert Elsmere,* very close to the author in temperament; and Marcella's school days are the most autobiographical bit found anywhere in Mrs. Ward's work. Marcella is headstrong, foolish, lovable, believable.

The plot is complex but unified. Marcella Boyce, her mother, and her father return to Mellor Park, the family estate, upon the death of her uncle. Marcella has been away from her parents, in schools, most of her life. The last two years before the "homecoming" were spent in London, studying art and music. Here she made the acquaintance of Anthony Craven, melancholy, suspicious, crippled older brother of Edith Craven, a fellow art student; and Louis Craven, the handsome younger brother, who was for a time hopelessly in love with Marcella. The Cravens are dedicated "Venturists" (Fabians) and did their best to convert Marcella. As Marcella looks out over her new "domain," she plans to put into action some of the Venturist ideas by improving the village belonging to Mellor Park. It has been sadly neglected by her misanthropic uncle. Marcella has never understood her mother's coldness toward her, the rare holidays at home, or the family's poverty. However, when their neighbors, Lord Maxwell, his sister, Miss Raeburn, and his grandson, Aldous, do not call, she learns the story of her father's infidelity to his wife and his participation in a financial scandal that ruined his reputation and broke his father's heart. He had been his father's favorite, generally bright and attractive, but selfish and shallow. His older brother's natural dourness was intensified by the "favorite's" betrayal of the family.

Marcella finds allies in Mary Hardin and her brother, the rector of the village church, and in their home meets Aldous Raeburn. The Maxwell family changes its attitude toward the Boyces when it recognizes the depth of Aldous's attraction to Marcella. When Aldous proposes, Marcella accepts, although she knows she is not in love with him. She reasons that as a "great lady" she can do much good. Then one of the families she is interested in dramatizes the conflicting ideologies represented. Mr. Hurd is a dwarf who has suffered much at the hands of Lord Maxwell's gamekeeper, Westall. Mrs. Hurd, a former lady's maid, has been more responsive to Marcella than most of the villagers. Of the three children, the oldest is a boy dying of asthma. Through Marcella's concern the Maxwells have given Hurd work, but he cannot give up the excitement of poaching, once necessary to feeding his family, still a satisfying proof of his manly skill. One night when Hurd is poaching with men from a neighboring area, Westall is killed and his teen-age helper badly beaten. Hurd is caught and convicted. Marcella will not agree with Lord Maxwell that the crime is murder and works with the Liberals to get a petition for Hurd's pardon. When the Maxwells will not sign the petition, she breaks her engagement to Aldous.

Volume two begins after Marcella has established herself as a nurse in London; Mrs. Hurd and the children live with her in a cheap but respectable apartment. She pays Mrs. Hurd something for maid service, and Aldous has given Mrs. Hurd a pension. Harry Wharton, an attractive, dynamic Liberal, whom Marcella's father had had as a guest at Mellor Hall while he campaigned against the Maxwell candidate for the district, is now the heir apparent to leadership of the Liberal party. When he needs a reporter who can turn in effective copy on the miners' strike, for his paper the *Clarion,* he acts on Marcella's recommendation and hires Louis Craven. Louis's work is so effective that the mine owners finally arrange a carefully handled bribe to rescue Wharton from bankruptcy and silence his paper. In the meantime, Marcella is injured in an attempt to protect a woman against her drunken husband. At the moment that the fight is discovered, Aldous Raeburn is inspecting the area as part of his duty as Under Home Secretary. He assists Marcella and takes her to Lady Winterbourne's home to recuperate. Marcella has begun to realize her feelings toward Aldous, but he acts with great coolness. At a party she attends with Lady Winterbourne, she meets Wharton and he proposes. She visits Edward Hallin, a friend of Aldous and the dedicated but dying "mind and heart" of the Liberals. Edward and his sister live in the area Marcella has been serving as a nurse. Edward tells her Aldous still loves her, and she confesses to him that she now loves Aldous. Aldous is with Edward when he dies, but Edward has lost the power to speak and so cannot tell Aldous of Marcella's confession. Wharton's acceptance of the bribe is uncovered by those in his party who oppose his leadership, but he comes to Marcella for an answer before she can learn of the situation. She now has the spiritual maturity to refuse him and pity him. Marcella's father dies, and Aldous is appointed executor of the estate. Other complications are cleared away and Aldous and Marcella are happily reunited.

The true incident upon which Mrs. Ward's imagination built this novel was related to their home Stocks, which the Wards saw for the first time in January of 1892. In the preceding December two gamekeepers in the employ of a neighboring landowner had been murdered by poachers. Before the Wards moved into Stocks in the late summer, the men had been convicted and executed, despite a strong effort for a reprieve. About her use of fictionalized facts Mrs. Ward wrote in the introduction:

> Yet, let it be understood, that when the murder came to be worked out in the novel, scarcely a circumstance of the original event remained. Westall and Hurd had no prototypes in real life. The actual men concerned in the Aldbury murder, and the incidents of the attack on the Pendley gamekeepers were different from anything described in *Marcella*. And I cannot insist too strongly that the book would have had no power and no illusion whatever, as romance, had it been otherwise. For as with the painter, so with the writer. Until the stuff of what we call real life has been re-created and transformed by the independent, possessive, impetuous forces of imagination, it has no value for the artist. . . .[2]

Furthermore, until the writer breathes into reality the flesh and blood, passion and heartache of romance, the sordid facts are only statistics in the centuries-old battle with the entrenched injustice of the game laws. The uneven battle of the poor with the legalized selfishness of the landed gentry is vividly dramatized for most Englishmen and Americans by the stories of Robin Hood and the Sheriff of Nottingham, a legend of the twelfth century!

Several other figures and incidents besides those related to the main incident of the murder and trial grew out of the village of Aldbury, located half a mile from Stocks. The old woman who had attended the plaiting school in her youth; the postmaster, who was a "chronicle" of the neighborhood; and an eighty-nine-year-old "Mrs. Jellison" are some of the real people the author wove into her story. The general scenery was drawn partly from the Hampden country, and partly from the neighborhood of Stocks. The scene on which Marcella looks out in the opening pages—a long falling avenue, two ruinous gate-houses at the farther end, the wild Chiltern uplands to the west and south of Hampden, and the lanes along which travelled the wood-carts loaded with beech-trunks—was part of the Ward family's enjoyment of the beautiful dismantled Hampden house in the summer of 1889. Portions of the house had been built in Elizabethan times; and a century later, couriers had brought news from London to the master of Hampden and his Cromwell kinsfolk, at Chequers. The chair makers still built their huts in the woods for convenience to the first processes of their work. Such a setting could hardly escape the pen of a novelist.

The various strains of social theory she introduces are those she met in the early days of her work with University Hall. The Fabians and their essays were the talk of the "various types of men and women who feel the shame of our social miseries and are driven thereby to some persistent effort to mend them."[3] Her reaction to the workers of city and village is reflected in a letter written to her father in September 1890.

> . . .Beatrice Potter told me that she had stayed for some time incog. as one of themselves with a family of mill-hands at Bacup, and that to her mind they were "the salt of the earth," so good and kind to each other, so dilligent, so God-fearing, so truly unworldly. She attributed it to their religion, to those hideous chapels, which develop in them the keenest individual sense of responsibility to God and man, to their habit

of combination for a common end as in their Co-op. Societies and Unions, and to their real sensitiveness to education and the things of the mind, up to a certain point, of course. And certainly all that I saw last autumn bore her out. . . .

The sincerely concerned men and women who were driven to attempt reform she captures in such characters as the Cravens, Marcella, Aldous, and Edward Hallin; the saintly poor she lovingly portrays in Mrs. Jervis and her family. But because Mrs. Ward is both romantic and realistic, the seamy side of the poor is given—Mrs. Hurd spoils our sympathy for her by complaining and weeping too much, and Mrs. Westall is unlovely even to her own mother. Mrs. Ward is quite sure that their aspiration can go only "up to a certain point," but she is impressed with their compensatory "sense of humour."

Amazing! Starvation wages; hardships of sickness and pain; horrors of birth and horrors of death; wholesale losses of kindred and friends; the meanest surroundings; the most sordid cares—of this mingled cup of village fate every person in the room had drunk, and drunk deep. Yet here in this autumn twilight, they laughed, and chattered, and joked—weird, wrinkled children, enjoying an hour's rough play in a clearing of the storm! Dependent from birth to death on squire, parson, parish, crushed often, and ill-treated, according to their own ideas, but bearing so little ill-will; amusing themselves with their own tragedies even, if they could but sit by a fire and drink a neighbour's cup of tea.[5]

A modern reader may find her opening sentences stereotyped and effusive, but they are quite properly romantic and typically late-Victorian. "The mists—and the sun—and the first streaks of yellow in the beeches—beautiful—beautiful! And with a long breath of delight Marcella Boyce threw herself on her knees by the window she had just opened, and propping her face upon her hands, devoured the scene before her with that passionate intensity of pleasure which had been her gift and heritage through life."[6] Mrs. Ward was capable of a swifter, more connotative style, especially in her interior settings which she successfully related to character or plot. Marcella discovers the portrait of one of her ancestors, an Italian lady of high birth whom one outstanding earlier Boyce had had the good fortune to marry. She decides that she and her father inherit their looks and talents from this lady, whose music books still occupy the room of the portrait; and upon this assumption Marcella justifies her dreams of becoming a great lady, even to her acceptance of Aldous's first proposal. Mrs. Ward rather neatly closes the earlier incident in this manner: "The Italian wife bore her lord two sons, and then in early middle life she died—much loved and passionately mourned. Her tomb bore no long-winded panegyric. Her name only, her parentage and birthplace—for she was Italian to the last, and her husband loved her the better for it."[7] Another setting that supports the plot is that of the dark, moonlit hall in which Marcella thinks to discover Mellor Park's ghost but instead encounters Harry Wharton; the two of them see Hurd sneak across the limits of the property on his way to poaching—and murder—and Wharton commits the Victorian offense of kissing Marcella, who is engaged to Aldous Raeburn.

Aldous Raeburn, destined to become an ideal landlord, husband, and government figure, is the man of two spiritual heritages—the Christ-like and the aristocratic. He is staid, even colorless, but absolutely essential, not only to the happiness of a woman like Marcella but also to the progress of his country. The necessary catalyst for such a pillar of British greatness is Edward Hallin, the "saint" of this novel, and the successor to Professor Henry Grey of *Robert Elsmere* and Ancrum of *David Grieve.* Aldous and Edward met at Cambridge. Edward, son of "an able factory inspector, well known for his share in the inauguration and revision of certain important factory reforms" and from whom Edward "inherited a passionate humanity of soul," was attending the university on a small scholarship. He soon proved himself a leader among the best of his fellow students, but had to relinquish the dream of honors his brilliant intellectual endowment placed almost within his grasp because of his frail physique. "After an inward struggle, of which none perhaps but Aldous Raeburn had any exact knowledge, he laid aside his first ambitions and turned himself to another career. A couple of hours' serious brainwork in the day was all that was ever possible to him henceforward. He spent it on the study of history and sociology, with a view of joining the staff of lecturers for the manufacturing and country towns which the two great universities. . . were beginning to organize."[8]

Hallin is successful for a number of years in his dual role of lecturer and inspiration for the Liberals who are sincerely dedicated to reform. When he dies, Aldous and Marcella are ready to take on the responsibility for fulfilling Hallin's dreams. Mrs. Ward describes this friendship thus:

The interest to which Hallin's mind soon became exclusively devoted—such as the systematic study of English poverty, or of the relation of religion to social life, reforms of the land and of the Church—overflowed upon Raeburn with a kindling and disturbing force. Edward Hallin was his gadfly; and he had no recourse, because he loved his tormentor.[9]

The heroine, Marcella, whose love is to give Aldous the happiness he so richly deserves, had Pre-Raphaelite beauty, a type of beauty characteristic of many of Mrs. Ward's heroines. Furthermore, she has qualities seen as especially feminine and compensatory for the lack of disciplined education men ought to have. Aldous describes Marcella to Edward Hallin, early in the novel:

She may be twenty or rather more. The mind has all sorts of ability; comes to the right conclusion by a divine instinct, ignoring the how and why. What does such a being want with the drudgery of learning? To such keenness life will be master enough. Yet she has evidently read a good deal—much poetry, some scattered political economy, some modern socialistic books, Matthew Arnold, Ruskin, Carlyle. She takes everything dramatically, imaginatively, goes straight from it to life, and back again.[10]

Marcella's beauty and ability, her fire and ice, her knowledge and her ignorance, will all be purified and given proper direction by suffering, the "ordeal unto salvation" of the second volume. One night after a visit with a young alcoholic mother, Marcella is overwhelmed with her own mistakes and all the tragedies of life which she cannot set right.

She thought of Mrs. Jervis—the saint—so near to death, so satisfied with "grace," so steeped in the heavenly life; then of the poor sinner she had just left and of the agony she had no power to stay. Both experiences had this in common—that each had had some part in plunging her deeper into this darkness of self-contempt.

What had come to her? During the past weeks there had been something wrestling in her—some new birth—some "conviction of sin," as Mrs. Jervis would have said. As she looked back over all her strenuous youth she hated it. What was wrong with her? Her own word to Anthony Craven returned upon her, mocked her—made now a scourge for her pride, not a mere measure of blame for others. Aldous Raeburn, her father and mother, her poor—one and all rose against her—plucked at her, reproached her. "Aye! what, indeed, are wealth and poverty?" cried a voice, which was the voice of them all; "what are opinions—what is influence, beauty, cleverness?—what is anything worth but *character*—but soul?"[11]

Mrs. Ward then fills out the outlines of this spiritual experience with doctrines familiar from her "preaching" in *Robert Elsmere* and *David Grieve.* However, Marcella's moment of truth is more emotional than that of these masculine soul-searchers. After her reaction against the evangelical training of her school years—with youthful conviction that socialism and science were enough for mankind, she concludes that no sensitive, intelligent person could work with the poor or know people like Edward Hallin and his sister, "without understanding that it is still here in the world—this 'grace that sustaineth'—however variously interpreted, still living and working, as it worked of old, among the little Galilean towns, in Jerusalem, in Corinth. To Edward Hallin it did not mean the same, perhaps, as it meant to the hardworked clergymen she knew, or to Mrs. Jervis. But to all it meant the motive-power of life—something that to-night she envied with a passion and a yearning that amazed herself."[12]

When *Marcella* appeared, the critics found it an advance in depth, unity, and dramatic power over both *Robert Elsmere* and *David Grieve.* Many conceded the author's preeminence among the women writers of her generation, but some objected to her lack of humor and wit, faults emphasized by later critics. The French critic Sir Francis Jeune found some scenes the equal of any George Eliot produced.[13] This comparison to George Eliot was to become a frequent occurrence throughout Mrs. Ward's career, with some justification. More significantly, *Marcella* begins the long list of novels about the social class and political professionals that governed England, portraits that interested her reading public enough to assure her outstanding popularity then and that are justly cited today as essential to understanding the period.

II Sir George Tressady, *1896*

Marcella's popularity seemed to justify her continued life in a second novel, *Sir George Tressady.* During the writing of *Tressady,* Mrs. Ward carried especially heavy burdens of correspondence and speaking on behalf of the organization of University Hall; wrote the intensely emotional *Story of Bessie Costrell;* and underwent a painful and unsuccessful minor operation. Nevertheless she made her usual careful preparation for the social and political details of the novel. For several months Mr. Sydney Buston, a Liberal friend, helped her with the details of the Parliamentary situation, even drawing her a colored plan of the House and the division-lobbies. The bill under consideration was to be a Factory Bill, sponsored by Aldous Raeburn, now Lord Maxwell, and ardently worked for by his beautiful and popular wife, Marcella. To write correctly of the bill, Mrs. Ward "put herself to school to learn every detail of the system of sweated home work prevalent in the East End of London at that time; wading through piles of Blue-books, visiting the actual scenes under the guidance of a Factory Inspector, or of Lord Rothschild's Jewish secretary [a title referring to the predominance of Jews among the garment workers]; learning much from her Fabian friends, Mrs. Sidney Webb and Mr. Graham Wallas."[14] Mrs. Ward feared that the "load of politics" might prove too much for the book, but fifteen thousand copies sold within a week, and the reviews were predominantly cordial.

The novel begins with George Tressady's victory, by a narrow margin, in the election for the Market Malford Division of West Mercia. He arrives in Parliament in time to participate in the hotly fought battle over a Factory Bill, sponsored by the government (the party in power) but opposed by Tressady's party, which is led by Dick Fontenoy. The government is ostensibly led by Dowson, but actually by Lord Maxwell, whose peerage places him in the House of Lords. Not only do the selfish factory owners and conservative political interests resent the bill, but Fontenoy succeeds in stirring up the ignorant victims of the sweated home work system, who naturally fear the slightest loss of their meager income, even for a period of adjustment to better conditions. During the campaign George meets and finds his interest captured by pretty, spoiled Letty Sewell, a young lady determined to marry above her original limited station.

George and Letty marry; Letty and Lady Tressady do not get on well. Even George neglects his silly, selfish mother, until he learns that she is seriously ill. By accident he comes under the spell of Marcella. At her invitation, he visits the people the Factory Bill is designed to help, and bit by bit emerges from his former cynical attitude toward the poor and grows doubtful of his own party's position. In the meantime, Letty has been seeing too much of Cathedine, an older man with a bad reputation but with the power to get her some of the social invitations she wishes. She has no interest in George's political work except the social importance it gives her, but she is reluctantly falling in love with her husband. One evening after George and Letty have quarreled over her association with Cathedine, George goes to a Maxwell at-home; in a short visit with Marcella he is inspired to do the noble thing—vote for the Factory Bill. The next session he makes a speech and switches sides—his success is sensational. When he goes to say goodbye to Marcella, he cannot hide his feeling for her, the first ideal woman he has ever known.

Marcella is horrified to realize how her "pure" attitude and sincere interest have unwittingly used Tressady to help her husband, and have hurt his marriage of only a few months. She bends all her efforts to heal the wounds and help Letty grow into a better person. She urges her husband to send George to influence a wayward nephew. George goes and succeeds. She visits Letty, is reviled, but finally wins an avenue to further influence—Letty is flattered that Lady Maxwell humbles herself to her, but is chagrined that there was so little truth in her jealous imaginings. When Letty and George return to his district, where his mines have been suffering strikes, Marcella continues her work through carefully worded letters to Letty. Letty becomes kinder to her mother-in-law, who is dying, and attempts some charity in the community. Lady Tressady dies; the strike is broken; and Letty and George have a tender scene in which she confesses that she is pregnant. George begins to hope that his marriage may be worth the struggle to make it a success. The next morning, there is an explosion in the mine. George goes with the rescue team; while the first group found is being helped, George, the leader of the strike, and a third man push deeper into the mine. A new cave-in kills the third man and fatally wounds George, who makes his former enemy, the union leader, promise to take a message to Letty. His dying moments are glorified by a vision of Marcella and some vague reassurances that all will be well.

Mrs. Ward begins this novel without the usual scenery and carries it steadily along on excellent dialogue. Much of this dialogue is in the language of the common people, who in vignette after vignette tell the story of their wasted lives and of the brutality of an economic system that desperately needed reform. The lines of Letty, Lady Tressady, George, and Fontenoy are admirably fitted to characterization and situation. Only Marcella is unrealistic—divinely naive, an angel not only to the workers but to George, to Letty, even indirectly to Fontenoy—she becomes the author's ideal "great lady," the lady who inspires only the best in men and leaves to their capable hands the actual machinery of politics. Yet she is a very efficient person—one who can take charge of an accident, tell everyone just what to do in caring for the injured girl or her distracted sister, manage several households, entertain the high or the low, and appear queenly either at a concert or in a slum tenement.

The contrasting characters, Letty and Lady Tressady, are both among Mrs. Ward's best drawn characters, shallow and selfish, but vital and individual. Aldous plays only a walk-on part, but the reader is assured that he is the ideal statesman promised in *Marcella.* But how the author had the temerity to destroy George Tressady, her most effective hero to date, is hard to understand. He is so much more than the vehicle of her "argument" that the end of the story comes as a disappointment to the reader. No doubt the "issue" for the original readers was the sweated home work system used to augment the factories; for the modern reader it is the destiny of a man who acted at first under the inspiration of a beautiful woman, but later discovered he had a character of his own. Of course for Mrs. Webb the greatest value of the book lay in its dramatization of political and social issues; however, she wrote, "This story is very touching, and you have an indescribable power of making your readers sympathize with all your characters, even with Letty and her unlovely mother-in-law."[15] And Rudyard Kipling wrote, "I am delighted to have *Sir George Tressady* from your hand. I have followed him from month to month with the liveliest wonder as to how the inevitable smash in his affairs was to fall. . . ." Furthermore, while for most readers the novel's burden of sordidness cries out for a bit of comic relief, Kipling found reason to comment, "How splendidly you have done the lighter relief-work! 'Fifteen out of a possible twelve' has already been adopted as a household word by us, who have two babies."[16]

In addition to her improved use of dialogue, Mrs. Ward has succeeded in tightening the warp and woof of description and action. One quotation may suffice to show this new, tighter style:

> On a hot morning at the end of June, some four weeks after the Castle Luton visit, George Tressady walked from Brook street to Warwick Square, that he might obtain his mother's signature to a document connected with the Shapetsky negotiations, and go on from there to the House of Commons.
>
> She was not in the drawing-room, and George amused himself during his minutes of waiting by inspecting the various new photographs of the Fullerton Family that were generally to be found on her table. What a characteristic table it was, littered with notes and bills, with patterns from every London draper, with fashion-books and ladies' journals innumerable! And what a characteristic room, with its tortured decorations and crowded furniture, and the flattered portraits of Lady Tressady, in every caprice of costume, which covered the walls! George looked round it all with a habitual distaste, yet not without the secret admission that his own drawing-room was very like it![17]

The weakest scene in the novel is the final scene, of George Tressady's death in the mine. William James explained the apparatus of mystical vision as dependent upon previous religious training or experience—thus the Catholic visionary sees the Virgin or a saint. But Mrs. Ward's heroes had generally discarded all traditional creeds, scriptural or doctrinal authority, or personalized religious disciplines. From such a theological bank account she can bring forth little specific currency. She substitutes quotations of poetry, an exalted image of the woman he loved, then inexplicable light.

> "What is it? Something watches me. There is a sense of something that watches me. There is a sense of something that supports—that reconciles. If—*if*—how little would it matter! *Oh! what is this that knows the road I came—the flame turned cloud, the cloud returned to flame—the lifted, shifted steeps, and all the way!*" His dying thought clung to words long familiar, as that of other men might have clung to a prayer. There was a momentary sense of ecstasy, of something ineffable.

And with that sense came a rending of all barriers, a breaking of long tension, a flooding of the soul with joy. Was it a passing under new laws, into a new spiritual polity? He knew not; but as he lifted his sightless eyes he saw the dark roadway of the mine expand, and a woman, stepping with an exquisite lightness and freedom, came towards him. Neither shrank nor hesitated. She hurried to him, knelt by him, and took his hands. He saw the sweetness in her dark eyes. *"Is it so bad, my friend? Have courage—the end is near." "Care for her—keep me, too, in your heart."* He cried to her, piteously. She smiled. Then light—blinding, featureless light—poured over the vision, and George Tressady had ceased to live.[18]

Thus Marcella becomes fully an angel, but George Tressady's "Beatrice" has not led him to "Paradise," because neither believed in anything but the faint hope that the deceased lived on for a while in the memory of the living. Despite this ending—a sentimental betrayal of an intellectual faith—*Sir George Tressady* clearly demonstrates Mrs. Ward's ascending powers as a writer.

III The Story of Bessie Costrell, *1895*

The novel that interrupted the work on *Tressady, The Story of Bessie Costrell,* is unique among Mrs. Ward's novels not only because it was written in a single intense period of fifteen days, but because it called for no research, nothing more than the author's absorption in the tale her imagination wove from the tragic details of an incident that occurred in Aldbury, the village that furnished material for *Marcella.* The work is a novelette instead of a novel, and gains thereby from its simple, unimpeded movement. It is included in this chapter on social-reform fiction because its undeclared purpose is sympathetic understanding of those whom educational and economic reforms might help. Henry James wrote of this work: "I think the tale very straightforward and powerful—very direct and vivid, full of the real and the *juste.* I like your unalembicated rustics—they are a tremendous rest after Hardy's—and the infallibility of your feeling for village life."[19]

The story begins as John Bolderfield, at sixty-two, is finishing his lifetime of work for the Hill family; he is set apart in the village because he has saved a "small fortune." Eliza, his widowed sister-in-law, with whom he lives, is dying. She wants him to put his box of money in the bank or let Saunders, proprietor of the Spotted Deer, take care of it. But John dislikes Saunders and distrusts the bank. Earnestly Eliza advises him against leaving the money with his niece Bessie Costrell. However, after Eliza dies, John finishes his work, leaves the box in a cupboard at Bessie's, and goes on a long-planned vacation. A few months later, an aunt leaves Bessie a small legacy—six shillings a week. The sudden sense of pleasure in new "richness" leads Bessie into debt. Then, one day, she discovers that she has a key that fits the cupboard in which John's money is locked. She takes a little at a time, becoming a daily customer at the Spotted Deer, where she treats everyone because she enjoys the excitement and the companionship. She never gets drunk, but she craves drink.

Her undoing begins with a comment made about the sovereigns she pays with, unusual coins for one of her class. She becomes frightened and hurriedly returns home to count the money, trying to figure how long it will take her to repay her borrowings, from her "legacy." She is discovered by Timothy, her husband's renegade son by his first marriage. Timothy knocks her down and takes all but two gold sovereigns and one silver coin.

Much of the temptation that had led her to the Spotted Deer was her loneliness, for her husband, Isaac, is a melancholy, religious man, puzzled by many questions beyond his education or associations. He returns on the night of Timothy's attack, in a mood to be kind to Bessie. She cannot bring herself to shatter his softened mood with a confession of her guilt. But the next day her uncle John returns, learns the truth, and gets Saunders and Mary Anne Waller, a neighbor, to confront Bessie. Bessie tells Isaac the whole story, including Timothy's part in the crime. Isaac can think only of the disgrace to his name, and when Bessie comes a second time to plead with him, he threatens her with a stick. She retreats to her bedroom, writes a note, calls Isaac out of a troubled sleep, then jumps into the well. He calls for help but she is dead. Mary Anne Waller takes care of the embittered John, but insists that not even he shall say anything unkind of Bessie.

Despite Henry James's approving comments, other critics and friends differed in their opinions of Mrs. Ward's ability to portray the lower class individual. Her first attempt to make such characters significant was with the creation of Reuben and Hannah Grieve, in *The History of David Grieve.* These and subsequent peasants or village people seem drawn from the outside. They are alive, have some individuality, and are motivated by easily labeled fears or desires—but Mrs. Ward believed that they were quite different creatures from the complex, sophisticated men and women of the upper classes. Hence Bessie Costrell barely achieves personality. One senses the sincerity of her moments of motherly tenderness but is puzzled by the slightness of their influence. The author succeeds to a greater degree in portraying the emptiness of Bessie's life—although she has four children, a home to keep, a faithful husband, relatives and neighbors—the emptiness most educated people see in the lives of the uneducated. Bessie's situation dramatizes her class's need for companionship, for escape from humdrum duty, and for a realistic concept of "riches."

A more basic truth is used in portraying the "strong" John as actually very dependent upon the "weak" Eliza or Mary Anne. Isaac is the most complex character, one worthy of the main role in a Hardy novel but incompletely presented in this story. Mrs. Ward's strong Arnold prejudice against Dissenters—her grandfather thought of them as those who weakened the true church; her uncle saw them as uncouth Barbarians—colors Isaac's portrait, but her belief in individuality in matters of faith enables her to draw a sincerely seeking, spiritual temperament. It was listening to the Vicar's missionary friend, a High Churchman, that had led Isaac to a new tenderness toward Bessie. "Isaac, as a staunch Dissenter by conviction and inheritance, thought ill both of bishops and Ritualists. Nevertheless he had been touched; he had been fired."[20] And after the tragic conclusion of Bessie's story, Isaac felt so deeply his failure to show mercy to his wife that he could not bear to hear his minister speak of God's mercy. Nevertheless, in the years that were left him, when not overcome with melancholy, he found comfort in the "aspirations and self-abasements of religion," for, according to Mrs. Ward's closing "sermonette," "No human life would be possible if there were not forces in and round man perpetually tending to repair the wounds and breaches that he himself makes"—forces that she labels "Divine tenderness," "undying hope," and "some ultimate salvation."[21]

Mrs. Ward could not, as did Mrs. Elizabeth Gaskell, make a

true hero or heroine out of the uneducated; yet this attempt to tell their story rises above her usual idiom of vision in that no benevolent lord or lady steals the spotlight. The truthful simplicity of this tale of human weakness recommends its survival.

IV Daphne: *or* Marriage à la Mode, *1909*

Daphne, or *Marriage à la Mode* (its American title) grew out of Mrs. Ward's only visit to the New World. On March 11, 1908, Mr. and Mrs. Ward, Dorothy and a maid, Lizzie, sailed for the United States. Their American host, Mr. Frederick W. Whitridge, and Mr. Ward and Dorothy all undertook to screen Mrs. Ward from reporters; what copy she permitted the papers she insisted upon seeing and rewriting. On the whole she was warmly received, especially in Boston. She presented her paper *The Peasant in Literature* several times as a benefit for her London Play Centres, and was pleased with the £250 this earned. It was through Mr. Whitridge's friendship with President Theodore Roosevelt that she was a guest at the White House. Mr. Ward had to return to London before they began the Canadian tour out of which Mrs. Ward wrote *Canadian Born* or *Lady Merton, Colonist* (1910). *Daphne* reflects little of the "success" of her State-side visit.

Roger Barnes, an English "Greek god," is in America to acquire a rich wife, for his father's recent death has left him and his mother almost penniless and they are used to wealth. Since he has recently been jilted by Chloe Fairmile, he is not adverse to a loveless marriage. His uncle, General Hobson, unhappily follows him about trying to advise him. Roger is Hobson's heir, but this legacy is in the future and not large. He meets Daphne Floyd, an orphan with beauty, brains, and money, who has just treated a certain Captain Boyson badly. Her constant companion is a widow, Mrs. Verrier, who married a Jew for love, but found that when he was unacceptable in her social circles, love was not enough. She was persuaded by her mother to seek a divorce, but her husband committed suicide—at Niagara Falls. Now she finds herself unwelcome everywhere, until Daphne takes up her cause and by the power of her own beauty, personality and money makes a "proper life" of sorts for Mrs. Verrier.

Roger and Daphne are married. After three years, Roger feels a comfortable attachment to Daphne, and a passionate attachment to their daughter Beatty. They return to Heston, the family home in England, where Roger's mother and friends are incredibly provincial and inept in their reception of Daphne. As the new mistress of Heston, Daphne, whose taste in art is almost that of an expert, sets out to redecorate her home. Roger knows nothing of such things, and his mother is hurt because part of the "atrocities" were of her choosing. Chloe Fairmile has returned to the neighborhood, separated from her husband, and determines to recapture Roger, who proves a dunce in her hands. Daphne's patience with Roger gives way to jealousy and she plots to trap him with evidence that he loves Chloe as he has never loved her. She returns to America with enough evidence to secure a divorce decree, which is of course unrecognized by English law. When Roger tries to see her or his child, she hides from him. Then Beatty dies. Roger turns to drink and finally to living with a woman he cannot marry.

Mrs. Verrier, who knows she is dying, returns to Niagara Falls to spend her final months. She becomes a Catholic and leaves Daphne a note urging upon her the sacredness of marriage. While caring for Mrs. Verrier, Daphne meets Captain Boyson in the hotel lobby. He is now happily married and on his honeymoon. He tells her of the tragedy of Roger's life and urges her to return to England to do what she can for him. Arriving in England, Daphne goes to the home of Herbert French, Roger's earliest and best friend, and his American wife, Elsie Maddison. The Frenches arrange a meeting between Daphne and Roger, but when Roger sees Daphne, he demands to know if Beatty asked for him before she died; then he tells Daphne it is too late to mend their marriage. Daphne is properly heartbroken.

Previously Mrs. Ward had matched a mature woman with an immature man, or the reverse. In this novel she matches two immature people, but places all the blame for the failure of the marriage on the woman, labelling Daphne the "transgressor" in the final lines of the book. She presents as a representative of the English Church an archdeacon of such bad manners as to be a comic figure, only to insist that his opinion is still superior to Daphne's. She makes Daphne incapable of true friendship but Roger incapable of making an enemy. And she has Mrs. Verrier so anxious to redeem her broken marriage that she becomes a communicant of the Catholic Church in the hope that she might be reunited in an after life with her Jewish husband who committed suicide—a ludicrous confusion of theological concepts. Everyone is on Roger's side, including the perennial "saint," Herbert French, who is melodramatically aged by his dedication to the East End. The vicar stood "pipe in hand, before the hearth, clad in a shabby serge suit, his collar alone betraying him. French's white hair showed even whiter than of old above the delicately blanched face; from his natural slenderness and smallness the East End and its life had by now stripped every superfluous ounce; yet ethereal as his aspect was, not one element of the Meredithian trilogy—'flesh,' 'blood,' or 'spirit'—was lacking in it."[22] Not only is this saint apparently still an orthodox Anglican clergyman—rather than an unorthodox Robert Elsmere or Richard Meynell—but Mrs. Ward's desire to introduce the name and theory of George Meredith, whom she knew and admired, betrays her into an impossible image: the ethereal or bloodless man still has Meredithian "blood." Even more melodramatic are such scenes as Chloe's meeting Roger "by accident," Daphne's fainting when she catches Roger with Chloe's old letters, and Mrs. Verrier's return to Niagara Falls to die.

The scene between Daphne and the Archdeacon would compliment Mrs. Ward's skill at portraiture if its satire were not confused by her position in the "argument": everything Anglican is sacrosanct; even an educated American should be humble before this bastion of British traditions:

> For him Mrs. Barnes was just a "foreigner," imported from some unknown and, of course, inferior milieu, one who had never been "a happy English child," and must therefore be treated with indulgence. He endeavored to talk to her—kindly—about her country. A branch of his own family, he informed her, had settled about a hundred years before this date in the United States. He gave her, at some length, the genealogy of the branch, then of the main stock to which he himself belonged, presuming that she was, at any rate, acquainted with the name? It was, he said, his strong opinion that American women were very "bright." For himself he could not say that he even disliked the accent, it was so "quaint." Did Mrs. Barnes know many of the American bishops? He himself had met a large number of them at a reception at the Church House, but it had really made him quite uncomfortable! They wore no official dress, and there was he—a mere Archdeacon!—in gaiters. And, of course, no one thought of calling them "my lord." It certainly was very curious—to an Englishman. And Methodist

bishops!—that was still more curious. One of the Episcopalian bishops, however, had preached—in Westminster Abbey—a remarkable sermon, on a very sad subject, not perhaps a subject to be discussed in a drawing-room—but still—[23]

The subject he introduces is divorce. Daphne's restraint to this point is meritorious. Her outburst after the indignant cleric's departure is entirely fitting to her character and would under other circumstances have met with Mrs. Ward's approval.

"Daphne!—my dear! what is the matter?" cried Lady Barnes, in dismay.

"He spoke to me impertinently about my country!" said Daphne, turning upon her, her black eyes blazing, her cheeks white with excitement.

"The Archdeacon!—he is always so polite!"

"He talked like a fool—about things he doesn't understand!" was Daphne's curt reply.

. . . .

"If he chooses to think America immoral and degraded because American divorce laws are different from the English laws, let him think it!—but he has no business to air his views to an American—at a first visit, too!" said Daphne passionately, and, drawing herself up, she swept out of the room, leaving the others dumfoundered [*sic*].[24]

How like Marcella Boyce, or Kitty Bristol, or Lady Connie, or Elizabeth Bremerton, or Pamela Mannering, she sounds, except none of these others made the mistake of being Americans! For the issue of divorce that is central to *Eltham House* (1915) seems to trouble the author not at all. One wonders if Mrs. Ward knew and perhaps disapproved of the famous American beauty—with beauty so like that Mrs. Ward gives most of her heroines—Consuelo Vanderbilt, whose mother forced her, in 1895, to marry, at eighteen, England's Duke of Marlborough. The Duchess of Marlborough did her duty for eleven years; then in 1906 (three years before the writing of *Daphne*) Consuelo rebelled, plunging into social work, horrifying her royal in-laws by running for office and winning. Since she did not obtain a divorce and marry Jacques Balsan, dashing pioneer of French aviation, until 1921, perhaps Mrs. Ward did not recognize this real life Daphne. Certainly she gave Daphne no "redeeming" social concerns, and the novel no affirmative "message." At least part of the intensity of Mrs. Ward's reaction to the American divorce laws—a reaction that seems to have warped her usual balanced point of view—was related, according to her daughter Janet Trevelyan, to the rising tide of suffrage for women, about which she wrote a somewhat better novel, *Delia Blanchflower.*

V Delia Blanchflower, *1914*

As early as 1889 Mrs. Ward had helped to organize a suffrage protest signed by eminent women of the world of education, literature, and public service, and published in the *Nineteenth Century.* Upon her return from America, she lent her distinction to the organization of a Women's National Anti-Suffrage League. By some unexplained twist of logic she believed that women should have voting rights in municipalities and membership on boards and committees where they might implement their ideals by good works. Janet Trevelyan says of her mother: "Decidedly Mrs. Ward was no democrat. She was willing to wear herself out for Mrs. Smith, of Peabody Buildings, and her children, but she could not believe that it would do Mrs. Smith any good to become the prey of the political agitator."[25] Her Anti-Suffrage activities culminated in the writing of *Delia Blanchflower,* begun in 1913. She believed that circulation of her books suffered from her unpopular stand, but the controversy was soon forgotten in the united effort of the war. Mrs. Ward was unstinting in her praise of women's new role in almost every essential effort—farming, munitions, administration—and she accepted gracefully the attendant change in suffrage—the right to vote was given British women in March of 1918.

Mark Winnington, the hero of *Delia Blanchflower,* is a delightful example of her traditional hero—forty, a perfect gentleman, loved and respected by everyone, full of good works, especially gracious to women. He becomes the guardian of beautiful twenty-two-year-old Delia, who has absorbed militant suffragism from Gertrude Marvell, a keenly intelligent, refined woman of the lower class who was cheated out of marriage by her own sister. Upon receipt of a legacy, Gertrude educated herself and won the position of tutor to Delia, who is also of above average intelligence. Delia is determined to give her fortune to Gertrude and the Daughters of Revolution. Monk Lawrence, a beautiful treasure house of English history, is the property of Sir Wilfrid Lang, the Daughters' bitterest enemy.

When Gertrude and Delia pass it on their way to Maumsey Abbey, Winnington's home, Gertrude's immediate desire to destroy Monk Lawrence draws a protest from Delia.

Lady Tonbridge, charming widow and a neighbor of Winnington, feels doubly obligated to assist him in managing Delia, for not only is she a friend of many years, but she is the one who recommended Gertrude to Delia's father; also, she is a suffragist of the right sort, ideologically and patiently. By the time Winnington has paid some of Delia's unwise debts, and Gertrude has not only begun to shut Delia out of the inner circle of the Daughters, but the "march" on the opening day of Parliament also has failed, Delia is disillusioned and struggling with her changed feelings toward her guardian. Paul Lathrop, an artist with a profligate background, sells Delia's jewels for her, but treats her honorably. He even wins Winnington's respect as they fight together to save Monk Lawrence. Gertrude and her confederate, Marion Andrews, outwit all precautions and destroy the landmark; in the holocaust Gertrude and the crippled little daughter of the caretaker die. Delia's early vows of loyalty to Gertrude are completely dissolved and she is free to give her heart and hand to Winnington.

The novel is outstanding in the development of many secondary characters—Gertrude Marvell, Lady Tonbridge, Miss Dempsey, Marion Andrews, Miss Toogood, Kitty Forster. Only Gertrude occupies the stage long enough to demand development, yet each is clearly delineated. Kitty is "a strapping girl, with a huge vanity and a parrot brain. A year before this date a 'disappointment' had greatly embittered her, and the processions and the crowded London meetings, and the window-breaking riots into which she had been led while staying with a friend, had been the solace and relief of a personal rancour and misery she might else have found intolerable."[26] Marion Andrews at thirty-four has had the most frustrating life—a selfish mother, an ineffectual brother, no education, no money, no future. Lady Tonbridge and her daughter are charmingly informal and impertinent; while Miss Dempsey—also a suffragist of the proper sort—is tall, awkward, old-fashioned, near-sighted and dowdy, but militantly independent and a "saint" whose fifty years of private "rescue work" in Latchford, a nearby city, have not made her "sweet" or "saintly."

This is the last of Mrs. Ward's novels that need to be labeled didactic, and while her point of view—anti-woman suffrage—was soon to be a "lost cause," she focuses so effectively on the people involved in rebellion against the status quo that the novel outlives its current event. Not only is she sympathetic to her "opponents," but she also succeeds in portraying the mixed motives of protest, the individuals that make up the masses—that make history. This talent for creating characters and portraying their reactions to each other and to ideological or social conditions was her true strength rather than the issues that she sought to promote, despite the publicity these controversial themes brought her.

CHAPTER 4

The Romances

IN a sense all of Mrs. Ward's novels are "romances," in that each has characters who are or become lovers or husband and wife. Some of the stories have more than one set of lovers; some have "triangles." And no matter what momentous affairs of state or church determine the climate of the adventure, the author is more concerned with the persons than with the issues of the conflict. However, when her didactic purpose is fully subordinated to her interest in variations on the old familiar themes of romantic love, Parliament and salons, country houses and Italian villas set the stage, but the author and the reader are absorbed in the tragedies and triumphs of men and women in love. Her very first novel, *Miss Bretherton* (1884), is such a romance, with a beautiful young actress and a scholarly English gentleman learning that even French training and London stage triumphs are not as important as the affair of their hearts. Appearing four years before her fame-producing novel, *Robert Elsmere, Miss Bretherton* attracted little attention but in retrospect reveals many of the techniques and interests found in all Mrs. Ward's writing.

I Miss Bretherton, *1884*

Isabel Bretherton has become the sensation of the London theater largely because her beauty perfectly suits her to her first role there. Eustace Kendal, scholar and esthete, considers her beauty to exceed her talent, but falls deeply in love with her. His sister Marie, Madame Chateauvieux, helps Isabel master the skills that reveal how great her talent really is. As Mme. Chateauvieux is dying, she sends Eustace to Isabel with a gift, and the promise that he will confess his love. Isabel is surprised but decides that she needs Eustace as much as he needs her.

Other characters that people Isabel's world and foreshadow Mrs. Ward's many secondary character creations are Forbes, the elderly artist who "worships" Isabel's beauty and opposes Eustace's Francophile standards; Edward Wallace, the American playwright whose play *Elvira* becomes Isabel's triumph; Mrs. Stuart, Edward's sister and Isabel's best London friend; and the Worrals, her aunt and uncle who are exploiting her beauty and success.

Charles Dudley Warner, editing *A Library of the World's Best Literature* (1897), says of *Miss Bretherton,* "It was a charming and thoroughly well-done piece of fiction, revealing marked ability in character study, and a comprehension of English society. . . . The writer of the later and greater novels is foreshadowed if not fully confessed in the tale."[1] Mrs. Ward was herself critical of this novel, which, she explains in the introduction to the 1909 edition, shows the first effect of London on her "academic inexperience," the conflict of her own passion for French belles-lettres with the chaotic, undisciplined public opinion of England's leading city. More specifically, an actual experience launched her imagination, a pattern of development common to many of her novels. She acknowledges that like many theater-going Londoners she had fallen under the spell of Miss Mary Anderson, an American actress whose radiant beauty "was accompanied by a simplicity, truth, and high-mindedness of nature which took the town by storm." However, the Wards had in 1874 seen Madame Bernhardt, as Phèdre, at the Théâtre Français, and they agreed with Henry James on "the general inferiority of the English theatre to the French, then undisputed and indisputable—[because of] the stress laid by English audiences on physical beauty and personal charm, as compared with the stress laid by French audiences on trained resource and artistic intelligence."[2] After entertaining Miss Anderson in her home, she and her husband and Henry James attended a performance that gave confirmation to their opinion that the relatively untrained actress would have benefitted from French dramatic discipline.

Eustace Kendal, her first hero, is understandably her most bookish, for she is still very close to her Oxford days. As her heroes change from minister, to bookseller, to M.P., to artist, to engineer, and to forester, their scholarly resources vary, but "literate" each must be. However, Kendal's serious occupation is writing—writing still unpublished, but scholarly, and he hopes, significant. She describes his study—the first of many such settings—with an awkwardness that she would outgrow: "The bookcases on the walls held old college classics and law-books underneath, and above a miscellaneous literary library, of which the main bulk was French, while the side-wings, so to speak, had that tempting miscellaneous air—here a patch of German, there an island of Italian; on this side rows of English poets, on the other an abundance of novels of all languages—"[3] There are unquestionably bits of excellent writing, but rarely a sustained section of choice prose, even more rarely *le mot juste* she was so aware of in French literature.

Kendal is the central figure, more than the heroine for whom the book is named. The story of his tardy awakening to the manliness and passions of love is told with the perceptive insight Mrs. Ward felt was the special strength of the woman novelist. In the preface to Smith and Elder's Haworth Edition of the Brontë novels, Mrs. Ward explains some of the genius of these famous chaste but passionate sisters by the fact that two of the talents required for novel writing have always been of prime concern to women—the art of speech, and the subject of love. "There are a hundred subjects and experiences from which sex debars them. . . . The one subject which they have eternally at command, which is interesting to all the world, and whereof large tracts are naturally and wholly their own, is the subject of love—love of many kinds indeed, but pre-eminently the love between man and woman!"[4] Kendal's metamorphosis provides the real conflict of the drama, for whereas Isabel Bretherton is young and eager to learn, Eustace Kendal is already set in his ways. Furthermore, her success can bring only bitter joy to the man whose advice she had taken so sweetly and effectively. Like all of Mrs. Ward's heroes, Kendal is a man as a woman sees him, more romantic than he is likely to think himself, despite the propriety and gentility of the 1870s.

Other precedent-setting qualities of this novel are the beauty of the heroine, the "great lady" traits of Mme. Chateauvieux, the awareness of outdoor scenery, the artful conversation and manners of the salon, the interest in the heroine's attire, the competitive social world of London. Mrs. Ward was thirty-three when she wrote this first novel. Perhaps because she was more mature than most novelists when they make their debut, this first novel is distinctly hers, a perfect piece of the great mosaic she was to construct through thirty books, as a monument to the world she knew and loved. Yet it has the freshness of a "first": the uncomplicated charm of all the characters, the idyllic Oxford scenes, the vicarious moments of triumphant theater, all make this a novel for youth, to be cherished as one cherishes memories of the first reading of *Lorna Doone* or *Jane Eyre.*

II Eleanor, *1900*

Eleanor is the first of her novels based on a famous true "romance"; its germinal idea was found in the relationship of Chateaubriand (1768–1848), French writer, statesman, and lover; and Pauline, Comtesse de Beaumont (1768–1803), charming center of a circle of artists and thinkers. François René, Vicomte de Chateaubriand was forced to flee to England during the Reign of Terror. His wife, Célèste, whom he had married for financial reasons but whose fortune was less than anticipated, and his sister, Lucile, who was his early mentor despite her unstable personality, were both arrested because he emigrated, but they escaped the guillotine. During the last months of his stay in England, he earned a precarious living translating and teaching but enjoyed living with the Reverend John Ives, an Anglican clergyman and Hellenist. The Iveses' fifteen-year-old daughter Charlotte and the impoverished young French nobleman experienced an idyllic romance that was shattered when her parents learned that he was already married. On a number of occasions Chateaubriand claimed that this "lost" love was the only "true" love of his life. However, his affections were easily won but were seldom constant. His most famous liaison was with Madame de Beaumont.

Pauline de Montmorin was the daughter of one of Louis XVI's ministers. At eighteen she married the Comte de Beaumont but found him so incompatible that she returned to her family shortly after the nuptials. She was very ill, "spitting blood," when the rest of her family were executed by the Revolution. M. Joseph Joubert, wealthy man of letters, rescued her from her peasant cottage refuge and in 1800 assisted her in establishing her apartment in Paris as a center of brilliant conversation. When he met Chateaubriand and recognized his genius, he introduced the young writer to Madame de Beaumont's circle. It was they who persuaded Chateaubriand not to publish his *Le Gênie du Christianisme* until he had tried one part of it, the part least likely to upset the jittery authorities. *Atala*, that "part," was a great success; in the meantime, Mme. de Beaumont had leased a charming rural residence in which she and the young author might enjoy their love and revise the larger work. This working romance was first broken when Chateaubriand fell under the spell of Mme. de Custine, known for her beauty (her nickname was "Queen of Roses") and for the generous bestowal of her favors. There were to be many other affairs, but he was reconciled to Pauline when she followed him to Rome for her last days; he forsook all other interests to minister to her and wrote in praise of her after her death.

Mrs. Ward's heroine, Eleanor Borgoyne, is a chaste English version of Pauline de Beaumont; the hero, Edward Manisty, is a proper-English-gentleman version of Chateaubriand. Eleanor's rival, Lucy Foster, is a pious American version of Charlotte Ives, although her entrance into the situation hints at the affair with Mme. de Custine. Like Chateaubriand, Manisty has many literary and ecclesiastical friends and an abnormal sister. Likewise, his "great book" argues the significance of the Church, but it is never published. There are other similarities, but Mrs. Ward was creating a new romance, not simply fictionalizing history.

Eleanor Borgoyne, a widow just turning thirty, had lost a cruel husband and a precious two-year-old son in the same night. Because she was exhausted with caring for her husband in an illness resulting from his dissolute living, the servants persuaded her to leave his side and rest. In the night he took their child and jumped to the river below the villa. For eight years she mourned. Then she began to help her cousin, Edward Manisty, write a book, a book attacking the "new" Italy and its attempt to separate civil and clerical power. Manisty enjoyed the company of elite church dignitaries, saw only destruction and corruption in the civil cause, and with aristocratic contempt—for religion was to him superstition except as it preserved art and tradition—he insisted that only the Church could manage the multitudes and sustain an orderly, moral world. He even turned on his good friend Father Benecke, a university professor, maintaining with the Church authorities that it was wrong to publish a book, no matter how true, if it undermined the power of the Church.

Aunt Patti Manisty is the other member of this cosmopolitan

household, situated twelve miles from Rome, into which the beautiful but unsophisticated Lucy Foster, an American friend of Aunt Patti, intrudes during her first European tour. Lucy's Uncle Ben had told her to enjoy herself, to dress well, to try new ways; but her strict Protestant, evangelical rearing, her keen mind and her strong character keep her plainly dressed and resistant to Italy's voluptuous and decadent beauty. At first Manisty ignores her, but Eleanor expresses her own deep need to love and serve by persuading Lucy to restyle her hair and wear clothes that will reveal her loveliness. At this juncture, Vanbrugh Neal, a professor friend, arrives and kindly but stubbornly tears apart Manisty's book. With the moodiness of a "genius," Manisty drops both the book and Eleanor, who had become a bit too helpful in the project. Then he discovers Lucy! His mentally unbalanced sister makes a surprise visit and attempts to kill Lucy to rescue her from loving Manisty. When Eleanor realizes the strength of Manisty's feeling for Lucy, she reveals her heartbreak to Lucy and the two "run away." For six weeks Manisty hunts. Although Eleanor is torn by a jealousy quite foreign to her nature, the affection of the two women deepens. Eleanor confesses her weakness to Father Benecke, the excommunicated but spiritually radiant priest. He, of course, counsels her to submit to suffering as a sign of God's love. She rebels; then one night she is mysteriously cleansed of all bitterness. The next morning she awakens happy, despite the knowledge that she has but a few weeks to live. The same day Manisty arrives in answer to a letter from Father Benecke. Lucy repulses him for what he has done to Eleanor. Eleanor triumphs over her own desires and "commands" Lucy to marry the man she loves. Before Eleanor dies she has a vision that testifies to her "rebirth" and acceptance, not of Father Benecke's "authority," but of the symbol of the crucifixion, a formerly hated childhood memory.

Janet Trevelyan says of the inspiration for *Eleanor* that her mother had decided she needed a really new setting and that she found herself still interested in Catholicism. In March 1899, Mrs. Ward and her family moved into the old Villa Barberini at Castel Gandolfo, in the Alban Hills. Despite the cold—there was a film of snow covering the ground the first night—and the strangeness of the Neopolitan cook and his dishes, the whole adventure was a success. One of their visitors was Henry James, who went with them on an excursion to the site of the famous temple of Diana

Nemorensis, on the shores of Nemi Lake, where they met "a beautiful youth at the *fattoria*, who for a few pence undertook to show [them] the fragments that remain. Mr. James asked his name. 'Aristodemo,' said the boy, looking as he spoke the Greek name, 'like to a god in form and stature.' Mr. James' face lit up, and he walked over the historic ground beside the lad, Aristodemo picking up for him fragments of terra-cotta from the furrows through which the plow had just passed, bits of the innumerable small figurines that used to crowd the temple walls. . . ."[5] This incident is recaptured in the novel: the visit to the temple and the terra-cotta figurines play their part in Manisty's discovery of Lucy. In one other way James seems to have influenced *Eleanor*, in his fluent friendliness with the Italian peasants. Mrs. Ward had been surprised and impressed; she wrote: "With the country people he was simplicity and friendship itself . . . the super-subtle, super-sensitive cosmopolitan found not the smallest difficulty in drawing out the peasant."[6] A similar skill is given Manisty, who "could always find a smile and a phrase for the natives. The servants adored him, and all the long street of Marinata welcomed him with friendly eyes. His Italian was fluency itself."[7] This observation is made by Jill Colaco in her refutation of the implication made by Leon Edel in his biography of Henry James *(The Treacherous Years*, 1969), that Mrs. Ward had caricatured James in the objectionable man of letters, Mr. Bellasis. Colaco suggests that Bellasis is drawn from the French poet Lamartine, whose visit to Mme. Récamier and Chateaubriand is reported in Sainte-Beuve's *Chateaubriand et son Groupe Littéraire* (1891; vol. 2), an incident which Mrs. Ward introduced into her novel to give excuse to show her hero's Chateaubriand-like impatience.[8] Certainly all other evidence would seem to indicate that Mrs. Ward sincerely admired Henry James.

In her *Recollections*, Mrs. Ward also identifies a specific incident as the basis for the story of Father Benecke. She was seated beside Cardinal Vaughan at a luncheon-party when the conversation turned to Doctor Schell, the Rector of the University of Wurzburg, who had published *Catholicismus und Fortschritt*, a plea on behalf of the Catholic universities of Bavaria and against the Jesuit seminaries which threatened to supplant them. The book had been condemned by the Congregation of the Index. Doctor Schell at first submitted; then, just before this luncheon, he withdrew his submission. "I saw the news given to the Cardinal. He shrugged his shoulders. 'Oh, poor fellow!' he said. 'Poor fellow!' It was not said unkindly, rather with a kind of easy pity; but the recollection came back to me in the crypt of St. Peter's, and I seemed to see the man who could not shut his ear to knowledge and history struggling in the grip of men like the Cardinal, who knew no history."[9]

The Countessa of *Eleanor* is Maria Pasolini, whose acquaintance the Wards had made in 1889. Of her Mrs. Ward says: "In her I first came to know, with some intimacy, a cultivated Italian woman, and to realize what a strong kinship exists between the English and the Italian educated mind. Especially, I think, in the case of the educated *women* of both nations. How an Italian lady manages her servants, and brings up her children; her general attitude toward marriage, politics, books, social or economic questions—in all these fields she is, in some mysterious way, much nearer to the Englishwoman than the Frenchwoman is."[10] Still another portrait, that of the Ambassador, is based on a real person, Lord Dufferin, who at a handsome sixty-five years of age managed English affairs in Rome. In 1892, on the occasion of an informal Christmas dance to which he had insisted the seventeen-year-old Dorothy Ward be brought, he showed his charm by claiming her first waltz. Mrs. Ward admits that the likeness was so closely drawn that before *Eleanor* was published, she sent him for his approval, the proofs of the scene in which "he" charms Lucy.

Eleanor is the most Jamesian of Mrs. Ward's novels. The essence of the novel is that same bloodless inner struggle of refined people so common to James. He was pleased with the book, writing: "I think her . . . a thing of rare beauty, a large and noble performance, rich, complex, comprehensive, deeply interesting and highly distinguished."[11] The characters are not involved deeply in any "issue," although Mrs. Ward cannot refrain from a judicious presentation of the good and bad in all religious positions, with the final emphasis on the rejection of authority and the acceptance of personal spiritual insights born in suffering. And Father Benecke is another "martyr" in the long struggle to enlighten religion with the author's "Holy Spirit"—History.

Stephen Gwynn, in *Writers of the Day* (1917), points out the novel's major strengths and the major weakness:

> If one places *Helbeck* at the head of Mrs. Ward's achievements, it must be allowed that *Eleanor*, which followed it, is equal to it in technical accomplishment, in completeness of design, and in the quality which most matters—sympathetic interpretation of the human heart. It is inferior, for reasons inseparable from the subject chosen. . . . In *Eleanor* the central male figure, Manisty, is a student of religious phenomena; he is the upholder of religious authority, not for the sake of religion, but for authority; because he sees it bound up with tradition, indispensable to civilized society. Essentially he is irreligious; and Eleanor is associated with him in his work, not for the sake of the work, but for the association. The story would have stood almost as well if Manisty had been writing directly on politics—[12]

More specifically, Mrs. Ward does not spare Eleanor the pettiness of her passion, and so strongly does Lucy contend for the center of attention that it is only after all is over that Eleanor dominates the reader's memory of the story. Consistent with the author's understanding of religion—a facet of individual personality—and her conviction concerning woman's role in life, Lucy is made to subordinate her originally strong religious convictions to the claims of love, although the only improvement in the "insufferable" Manisty is a new insight into the vitality of the Italian people and evidence that he is really in love for the first time in his life. And though Mrs. Ward describes the Italian setting with skill and appreciation, it remains a setting seen through the eyes of a tourist, not a resident. While Manisty's defense of Christianity as the creator and bulwark of man's aesthetic inheritance is close to Chateaubriand's position in *The Genius of Christianity*, Mrs. Ward's hero—with his handsome head, slight limp, and habit of standing behind a table or chair to display the head and hide the limp—seems to resemble Lord Byron, the English Romantic, rather than the French Romantic whose story sparked her original plot.

The success of the novel led theatrical friends to persuade Mrs. Ward to make a play of *Eleanor*. She and Mr. Julian Sturgis collaborated, working in a villa on the outskirts of Rapallo. When production promises failed to materialize, Mrs. Ward undertook the renting of a theater and the other necessary equipment. However, the play ran only fifteen matinees, October 30 through November 15, 1903, and saw only two special matinees, given in aid of the Passmore Edwards Settlement. Despite the financial loss, she enjoyed the experiment and tried it again with both the next two novels.

III Lady Rose's Daughter, *1903*

The story of two famous French hostesses, Mademoiselle Julie de Lespinasse and Madame de Deffand, stirred Mrs. Ward's imagination and produced *Lady Rose's Daughter*. Mme. Deffand took as her companion Julie de Lespinasse, who was actually the illegitimate half-sister of her brother's wife. The jealousy and cruelty of the older woman, the ambition and treachery of the younger, the discovery of Julie's unofficial use of the salon, her passionate love for the unworthy Comte Guibert, and the love of d'Alembert, the faithful and heartbroken friend who could not save Julie are paralleled in Lady Henry Delafield, Julie le Breton, Warkworth, and Jacob Delafield, except Jacob does "save" Mrs. Ward's Julie. The author felt later that she had betrayed the artistic conscience, but at the time her physical and mental state could not face "living through" the wretched end she had originally assumed Julie's character and temperament merited.

> At the bottom of my mind indeed was the conviction that Julie would in truth have destroyed herself, whatever Delafield might do. But this conviction was met by another equally clear—that I no longer had the nervous energy wherewith to do it. The thought of Julie, ruined and dying, of the wrestling with feeling and realisation which lay before me if I was to bring home to myself first, and to my readers afterwards, a tale at all akin to that which appears in the letters of Julie de Lespinasse—presented itself to me, as the thought of another rock-face to climb might present itself to one already worn out in a wrestle with the mountains.[13]

Actually the circumstances of Jacob's rescue of Julie are convincing, the gallant platonic marriage consistent with Jacob's character, and the entire subdued conversion of Julie's life more appropriate to English taste at the turn of the century than a closer copy of the earlier French situation would have been.

For many people Mrs. Ward's novels did for the England of her day and class what Dickens had done for his. The French critic Abel Chevalley says: "It will, for example, be very difficult hence forward to picture England at the end of the nineteenth century without recourse to the multiple and monumental image of it left by Mrs. Humphry Ward. Nothing more comprehensive, more intelligent, in every sense of these words, could be conceived."[14] The contribution of *Lady Rose's Daughter* to this panorama of England is the creators and habituées of the salon, an institution borrowed from the Italians and the French, and used as an instrument of political as well as social prestige by the English. The artistry of arranging rooms, the genius of securing guests, the brilliance of conversation are all superbly portrayed in *Lady Rose's Daughter,* with no issue to detract from this most sophisticated of adventures—the competition of beautiful women. The keenness of this competition Mrs. Ward describes through Julie. "Moreover, the gatherings themselves ministered to a veritable craving in Julie le Breton—the craving for society and conversation. She shared it with Lady Henry, but in her it was even more deeply rooted. Lady Henry had ten talents in the Scriptural sense—money, rank, all sorts of inherited ties and associations. Julie le Breton had but this one. Society was with her both an instinct and an art. With the subtlest and most intelligent ambition she had trained and improved her natural gift for it during the last few years."[15]

Added to these unforgettable protagonists is an array of fascinating minor characters: Sir Wilfrid Bury, Lord Lackington, the Duchess of Crowborough, Lady Blanche, and Warkworth; even deceased characters in the drama are interesting: Lady Rose; her husband, Colonel Delaney; her lover, Marriott Dalrymple; and an old cousin of the young Duchess. The descriptions of the homes of the English governing class and the Italian settings in which they found renewed life are well done. However, the most intriguing creation of the book is the hero, Jacob Delafield. At first he does not seem the hero, for Julie, Lady Henry, the Little Duchess, and various men of political importance hold the center of the stage. Jacob is there to introduce others, to do the bidding of the Duchess, to love and puzzle over Julie from afar. And while he reads some poetry, the Bible, Ruskin, Tolstoy, and other authors from Mrs. Ward's approved list, he is robust, active, an "Etonian, who could ride, shoot, and golf like the rest of his kin, who used the terse, slangy ways of speech of the ordinary Englishman, who loved the land and its creatures, and had a natural hatred for a poacher."[16] Yet he was a mystic, a man who rebelled against conformity to his class, who dreaded above all the position to which he was the obvious heir, a dukedom. Many people depended upon him, though most found him crotchety; he was awkward and sincere, in the end a good match for the heroine who had trained herself to social perfection but was passionate and insecure in her private life.

Two themes are skillfully woven into the novel. The first is the acceptance of class privilege as important to both social stability and personal happiness. Lady Henry, sixty-five, almost blind, and generally disagreeable, still has "rights" to her position as the social tyrant of her Wednesday evenings—rights neither the sympathetic reader nor Lady Henry's relatives and friends can give to the illegitimate Julie. Further, the real explanation of Julie's redemption is not so much Jacob's love as her acceptance by Lord Lackington, her grandfather. And despite Jacob's righteous rebellion against class hypocrisy, he must take up the burden of his inheritance as the Duke of Cudleigh. The second theme is the two sides of the religious issue that most appeal to Mrs. Ward—the unorthodox mysticism and good works of Jacob and his crippled tutor, Courtney; and the recurrent Catholicism of Julie, who had been educated by the Belgian nuns at Brugh. For the average man, like the ambitious rake Warkworth, there is some "survival of a moral code inherited from generations of scrupulous and God-fearing ancestors."[17] And this is called forth by the realization of the patriotic responsibility he has asked for in the eagerly sought appointment to the Mokembe Mission. Fortunately Warkworth does not survive to pass on his diluted religion to any heirs.

Most modern readers would agree with an early critic that in *Lady Rose's Daughter* Mrs. Ward achieved a "brilliance and vivacity . . . the easy touch and go of familiar talk, the delicate but sharply defined contrasts of character in appearance, bearing and speech . . . [even] lightness of touch, variety of mood and temperament"[18] not apparent in her earlier novels and only occasionally in later ones. And the dramatic intensity of the novel is attested to in the fact that not only was it made into a play, called *Agatha*, in 1905, but it was made into a movie, in 1920, by Paramount-Artcraft.

IV The Marriage of William Ashe, *1905*

The success of *Lady Rose's Daughter* encouraged Mrs. Ward

to use another well-known situation — that of William Lamb, Lord Melbourne, and his wife, Caroline, whose eccentric conduct verged on insanity — and play the tragedy out again with a new set of players, in contemporary conditions; the result was *The Marriage of William Ashe.* Later, Mrs. Ward was to cite as partial justification of her biographical fiction the fact that two of George Meredith's novels were derived from true stories — *Tragic Comedians,* based on the tale of Frederick Lassalle, and *Diana of the Crossways,* based on the legend of Mrs. Norton, who figured in the later life of the same Lord Melbourne. One of Mrs. Ward's settings — spring in Venice, records a month spent there by the author and part of her family in 1902. The setting for Kitty Ashe's death in the Simplon inn is based on an incident of a trip to Italy, in 1899. The party included a young maid dying of tuberculosis. The stay in Italy had helped her little, and on the return over the Simplon, she caught cold, so the travelers stayed at the old inn until she was able to go further. When she had recovered sufficiently, they took her on to England, where she died, early in the following year. It was her delicate, refined beauty, reports Mrs. Ward, that gave reality to the suffering of Kitty.

A comparison of the novel with the life of Lord Melbourne as told by Lord David Cecil, in *Melbourne* (1939), reveals that fiction and fact match at many points. Lady Melbourne's ambition was even greater than that of Lady Tranmore, her fictional counterpart. William Lamb was first attracted to Caroline Ponsonby when she was fifteen; he fell in love with her when she was seventeen, he twenty-four. William Ashe falls in love with seventeen-year-old Kitty Bristol. However, the real-life heroine, Caroline, as the only daughter of Lord Bessborough, was not permitted "to throw herself away upon the younger son of a small fortune."[19] So it was not until William's older brother, Peniston, died and William became heir to a peerage and that "small fortune," that either he or Caroline sought to defy the strictures of their class. Even then Caroline's mother hesitated — she did not like William's scepticism nor his mother's thinly disguised ambition; but she was anxious to get Caroline settled, and the two young people had been in love for two years. The exalted position of Caroline Ponsonby seems in striking contrast to the unsavory brew from which Mrs. Ward's heroine springs, until Cecil points out that Lady Bessborough's reputation was so tarnished that it was thought wise to have Caroline reared by her grandmother, Lady Spence, or with her cousins at Devonshire House. Neither household cared to pay the price of properly rearing this difficult child. The philosophy of Devonshire House set no value on reason or self-restraint, but held that passion and sensibility were the only virtues. Cecil describes the result: "Indeed she was the most dynamic personality that had appeared in London society for a generation." Her slight figure and childlike face and voice gave her the nicknames of "sprite" and "the Fairy Queen." "On fire for the dramatic, the picturesque, the ideal, openly at war with the tame and the trivial, at every turn she flouted convention."[20] She cast a spell upon many, even the friends and servants to whom she showed her most difficult sides. And she left in her correspondence evidence that suggests undisciplined genius. Kitty casts her spells, too; but Mrs. Ward in giving her a father strongly resembling "Mad Jack" Byron — father of the poet who figured so notoriously in Caroline Lamb's affairs and who is represented by Geoffrey Cliffe in the novel — seems to be offering some explanation for Kitty's "inherent evil."

The Lambs' subnormal infant son is equated with the Ashes' delicate, crippled son. The factual or historical episodes of the masked ball, the exposé novel, the several attempts at separation and other real incidents are retold in the novel. The conflict is shortened for artistic purposes and the climax of the relationship between Kitty and Cliffe, as well as the character and intrigue of the villainess, Mary Lyster, are fiction. However, the author has the audacity to have the Dean (one of her most successful "old men") suggest that Kitty be gently restrained in a country estate so that she will not ruin her husband's career because that is what Lord Melbourne did with his wife! Even more daring is the authenticity of Ashe's portrayal of Melbourne's attitudes. William Ashe is fascinated with Kitty and as deeply in love as he will permit himself to be. He wishes to rescue her from the soiled company of her mother, Madame d'Estrées, but he swears he will not try to reform her, though her youth and her temperament cry out for a strong man with unflagging interest in her development. William Lamb's biographer comments many times on Lord Melbourne's failure to command Caroline's respect and save her from herself—because his self-image would not permit him to become passionately involved in anything. Mrs. Ward describes Ashe as ironically critical of the world he definitely does not want to change.

> That a man should know himself to be a fool was in his eyes, as it was in Lord Melbourne's, the first of necessities. But fool or no fool, let him find the occupations that suited him, and pursue them. On those terms life was still amply worth living, and ginger was still hot in the mouth. . . . Religiously he was a sceptic, enormously interested in religion. . . . Politically . . . he was an aristocrat, enormously interested in liberty. . . . To have the reputation of an idler, and to be in truth a plodding and unwearied student; this, at any rate, pleased him. To avow an enthusiasm or an affection, generally seemed to him an indelicacy.[21]

But she has him grow under political responsibility as she was sure the best young English aristocrat would mature. Again she dares make her example explicit: "Lord Melbourne had begun his career as a person of idle habits and imprudent adventures, much given to coarse conversation, and unable to say the simplest thing without an oath. He ended it as the man of scrupulous dignity, tact, and delicacy, who moulded the innocent youth of a girl-queen, to his own lasting honour and England's gratitude."[22] In the light of Cecil's verification of William Ashe as a model Englishman, it is ironic that *Blackwood's Edinburgh Magazine* in a lengthy review insists that the hero "is an impossible character. He has married a self-willed child, scarcely more than half his age, out of a wretched home, given her wealth and high social position, and surrounded her with everything, including his own love, that she most values. Yet he is represented as a mere log of wood in regard to her, and is sedulously deprived of all control, or even influence, over the successive situations which arise, in a manner which one feels instinctively does not correspond with real life."[23] One wonders which is worse, this critic's prejudice against fictional husbands who do not exercise proper authority over their wives or his ignorance of one of his country's most famous statesmen.

The book is too long, and Kitty's purification in the revolting relationship to Cliffe juxtaposed to the suffering of the natives they have come to help is pure melodrama. But the author saw clearly the guilt of a society that helped to form both Kitty and an English gentleman who sacrificed his wife's spiritual maturation to protect his "image." The Dean's plea to William and his mother to go to Kitty after she has "fallen" is again Mrs. Ward's emphasis on redemptive human love. Some contemporary critics were shocked that Mary Lyster, the "wholesome," "normal" young woman William was supposed to have married, should stoop to betray Kitty into Cliffe's hands. Yet Kitty had taken both William and Cliffe away from Mary, a woman consistently portrayed as strong-willed enough to hold her own in political conversation, run her own business affairs, shut out of her life a sister who had made an unfortunate marriage, and maintain an enviable social position in a very competitive world. Once again there are the small but distinctive Ward touches—descriptions of the dress of all her female characters; dinner scenes in which food is never mentioned; the role played by women in the governing of a nation.

William Ashe was prepared for dramatization by Mrs. Ward and Miss Margaret Mayo, during 1905, and was used by an American stock company with some success in the States. However, in London, where it was performed by a semi-American cast, in 1908, "it fell very flat."[24] It ran only three weeks. Thereafter none of Mrs. Ward's plays were ever produced in England. Nonetheless, the play was made into a movie, in 1921, by the Metro Pictures Corporation.

V Fenwick's Career, *1906*

Mrs. Ward's next novel, *Fenwick's Career*, was also based to some extent on facts, this time on incidents in the life of the painter George Romney. Romney married, in his youth, a Kendal girl, whom he left behind him when he went to London to seek training and fortune. There he fell under the influence of Lady Hamilton and did not return to his wife in Westmoreland till thirty years later. She took him back and nursed him through his dying hours. This true life tragedy inspired Tennyson's "Romney's Remorse." Part of the original story's attraction for Mrs. Ward was its Westmoreland background. More specifically, Robin Ghyll, the Fenwick cottage, was the property of Mrs. Ward's daughter Dorothy. Mrs. Ward, Dorothy, and Aunt Fan Arnold drove up Langdale one summer day in 1902, saw the cottage, and fell in love with it. Two years later, when it fell vacant, Mrs. Ward leased it for Dorothy, as a retreat when her duties at Stocks could spare her. Her sister, Janet Trevelyan, writes: "Not often indeed could she be spared from the absorbing life of Stocks, or Italy, or Grosvenor Place, where so much depended upon her. But though life limped at Stocks during Dorothy's brief absences, she always returned from Robin Ghyll with strength redoubled for the arduous service of love which she rendered to her mother all her life long, and from which both giver and receiver derived a sacred happiness."[25] Her usual care in presenting other facets of the novel is typified by her making a visit to Versailles before writing the corresponding scenes in *Fenwick's Career*.

John Fenwick, an artist, accepts £200 from a Mr. Morrison as a loan to be paid back with copies of museum works or good originals. His wife, Phoebe, wants to go with him to London, but he feels he must be absolutely free to devote himself to art. Once there, a moment of uncertainty and embarrassment and continued silence on the matter give the impression that Fenwick is not married. He does the portrait of beautiful, wealthy Eugénie de Pastourelles, whose husband has deserted her. Phoebe comes to the studio, finds the portrait and some letters, destroys the picture, leaves a message for John, and disappears with their small daughter Carrie. John tries to find them, but fails. In the next few years he becomes successful, partly through the friendship and inspiration of Eugénie. Then Eugénie's husband returns to her to be nursed through his final illness. After a year of mourning, she and her father, Fenwick, and Arthur Welby, another artist, and Arthur's invalid wife, meet in Paris. Fenwick has always been jealous of and, therefore, rude to Welby. His bad manners on many occasions have cost him most of his early success. At Versailles he permits himself to begin to fall in love with Eugénie, and she somewhat encourages him, thinking it the only way to restore his talent. Belle Morrison appears and tells Welby that Fenwick is married. There follows confession, heartbreak, Fenwick's return to London and bitter defeat. One day he sees a girl he is sure is his daughter Carrie. Failing to find her, he attempts suicide. Phoebe, having returned to England after twelve years in Canada, sends him his self-portrait and a note. Eugénie visits Phoebe, telling her the truth and informing her of her husband's illness. In the same Westmoreland cottage in which their married life began, now owned by an old friend, they meet. John is unforgiving, but softens to his daughter's charms and finally husband and wife are reconciled

Mrs. Ward captures successfully the youthful love of Phoebe and John, John's changing needs, Phoebe's loneliness and jealousy, the response of the artist first and then the man to Eugénie's beauty and sympathy. But Eugénie is too completely the product of Mrs. Ward's dream world to survive in the company of her more vital heroines. Religiously, Eugénie is a free-thinker. She reads French and German criticism on religion and is strongly in sympathy with Arthur Welby, who is an agnostic. Yet she goes every morning to a little Ritualist church. When questioned by her father, Lord Findon, she replies, "It's an *Action*—not words—and an action means anything you like to put into it—one thing to me—another to you. Some day we shall all be tired, shan't we?—of creeds, and sermons, but never of 'This do, in remembrance of Me!' "[26] Later, when she is under the sense of guilt with regard to Phoebe, "Her soul, sorely troubled and very stern with itself, wandered in mystical ascetic paths out of human ken. Every morning she hurried through the woods to a little church beside the sea, filled with fishing-folk. There she heard Mass, and made the spiritual communion which sustained her."[27] Mrs. Ward notes in the introduction that the "drawing of Eugénie made perhaps my chief pleasure in the story";[28] so we must hold her responsible for this unearthly creature:

> More than ever was she a creature of tenderness, of the most delicate perceptions, of a sensibility, as our ancestors would have called it, too great for this hurrying world. Her unselfishness, always one of her cradle-gifts, had become almost superhuman; and had she been of another temperament, the men and women about her might have instinctively shrunk from her, as too perfect—now—for human nature's mundane qualities. Nobody knew her, luckily, for the saint she was; she herself least of all. As her strength renewed itself, her soft fun, too, came back, her gentle inexhaustible delight in the absurdities of man and things, which gave to her talk and her personality a kind of crackling charm, like the crispness of dry leaves upon an autumn path. Naturally, and invincibly, she loved life and living; all the high forces and emotions called to her, but also all the patches, stains, and follies of this queer world. . . .[29]

This bit of description is stylistically one of the best Mrs. Ward has done—but the character described is sentimentally Victorian, not the twentieth-century woman Mrs. Ward usually admired.

Janet Trevelyan writes of her mother's literary career: "I think that those two novels of London life, *Lady Rose's Daughter* and *William Ashe,* had marked its highest point in sheer brilliance and success; after these the long autumn of her novel-writing began, which, like all mellow autumns had its moments of more true and delicate beauty than the full summer had possessed. The first of these autumn novels . . . was *Fenwick's Career*. . . ."[30] It has to recommend it such choice scenes as those at the cottage, Fenwick's studio, and his emotional outbursts. The Versailles setting has been praised, but unwisely. The book reveals the author's careful workmanship, her usual interest in religion, her balanced realism and romanticism—but it contributes nothing to her stature as a novelist.

VI The Testing of Diana Mallory, *1908*

The Testing of Diana Mallory was dedicated to Mrs. Ward's American and Canadian hosts, but it reflects none of her New World experiences. Instead, the novel captures again the panorama of village gentry and the governing class, with a heroine, attractively modern, pitted against a "hard" fortune-seeking rival, a bigoted mother, and a weak lover. Diana Mallory returns to England, just before Christmas, thrilled to be "home" in England after living most of her life abroad with her father. She can barely remember her mother. She purchases Beechcote Manor and determines to love everything English. Mrs. Muriel Colwood, a refined young widow, becomes her companion. The Vicar disapproves of Diana's reading selections and the gossips are titillated by the freedom she gives her servants. Lady Lucy and her son, Oliver Marsham, who had met Diana and her father in Italy, welcome her to Tallyn Hall, Lady Lucy's home—a hideous manor built with "iron" money and atrocious taste. Isabel Fortheringham, Oliver's sister, who is a militant liberal in politics, stridently dislikes Diana's conservative, patriotic convictions. Alicia Drake recognizes Diana as a rival for Oliver, but plays a waiting game.

The day Oliver proposes he discovers Diana's mother was Juliet Sparling, convicted of murder when Diana was four. Sir James, close family friend, and Oliver plead with Lady Lucy, but she threatens to disinherit Oliver if he stains the family name by marrying Diana. Diana releases Oliver from the engagement, and he acquiesces because he has practically no income of his own. The "revised" story of Diana's mother appears in the papers, offering proof that the woman she killed—in self-defense— and the victim's husband, Sir Francis Wing, had been bleeding Juliet of her inheritance through gambling, seduction, and blackmail. Public opinion turns against Oliver. However, the Liberal party gets into power and Ferrier, Lady Lucy's best friend, is given the post of Minister of the Exchecquer; Oliver is allotted a minor post that necessitates his running for office again. The next morning the *Herald* prints some indiscreet words Ferrier spoke only to Oliver; Ferrier's appointment is withdrawn and he dies of a heart attack from the disappointment and the realization that Oliver had betrayed him. During the second campaign, in which Alicia participates as Oliver's fiancée, Oliver is struck by a colliery worker who is resentful of the mining abuses that fatten the Marsham fortune. Oliver's back is injured; his eyesight fails; the doctors insist that it is shock and will pass, but he grows worse. Then Alicia deserts him, and Lady Lucy begins to break under the strain. Diana invites herself back to Tallyn to relieve Lady Lucy. She finally insists that she and Oliver marry so that she may care for him always. The next day a new treatment brings promise of recovery.

There are several subplots, each successfully woven into this tapestry of English country life. Fanny Merton, Diana's coarse, tale-bearing cousin, arrives from Barbados, ostensibly to secure training to make herself self-supporting, but actually to bleed Diana for money and to marry; she becomes pregnant by an unprincipled solicitor whom Sir James makes marry her, and then he sends them both back to Barbados. More attractive are Bobbie Forbes, a protégé of Lady Niton, and his plain but fine fiancée, Ettie, for whom he is willing to give up his future in the Foreign Office and Lady Niton's help. But Lady Niton gruffly accepts Ettie and demands that he accept a better position that she has arranged for him. The doctor's son falls in love with Diana, goes away to military service, proves his worth and comes back to choose more wisely, marrying Muriel Colwood. Two "saintly reformers," Marion Vincent and Lankester, briefly preach Mrs. Ward's doctrines. But the didactic or serious subjects are lightly touched and some of the dialogue is better than usual. Sir James Chide joins the gallery of lovable old men; Lady Niton the wise, eccentric grand dames; and Diana, made of the now familiar combination of beauty and brains, liberal religion and capacity to love, succeeds in being the heroine of the novel. One reviewer commented, "It is not a great novel, but Diana is almost a great figure."[31] Another compares it favorably with *Fenwick's Career, The Marriage of William Ashe,* and *Lady Rose's Daughter.* "Judged by the test of originality, the book stands on a much higher plane than any of its three predecessors, while the story, regarded as merely a story, is at least as engrossing, as well furnished with incident, and as strong in dramatic interest."[32] Some of the critical comments reflect the growing boredom with Mrs. Ward's familiar material, yet generally there is still respect for her basic craftsmanship. "There is not a thrilling scene in the book, nor a single character of extraordinary fascination; but it is written with a fineness of perception, a delicacy of expression that redeems it from the commonplace."[33]

VII Lady Merton, Colonist *or* Canadian Born, *1910*

Growing out of Mrs. Ward's visit to Canada in 1908, the novel *Lady Merton, Colonist,* or *Canadian Born,* is strong on scenery and weak in plot. Elizabeth Merton, twenty-seven but a widow from ten months after her marriage, at nineteen, to Sir Francis Merton; Philip Gaddesden, her twenty-three-year-old brother, a young man of immature habits and delicate health; and Arthur Delaine, a forty-year-old English gentleman whose interests are antiquity, appropriate travel (that is, in Rome, Athens, and so on), and Elizabeth—all are traveling across Canada, in the spring, as the special guests of the Canadian Pacific Railway, of which Elizabeth and Philip's father was one of the founders. Philip objects to Elizabeth's enthusiasm for the scenery, her habit of wearing black, and her attempts to restrict his drinking. When the train is delayed for many hours by a sinkhole, they meet a young Scotch Canadian engineer, George Andersen, when he asks for the return of some milk secured from a nearby cow by the train's cook but needed by an emigrant baby. Elizabeth goes with George to deliver the milk; later George entertains Philip with stories of big game hunting.

George has risen by intelligence and fine character above an early tragedy. When he was eighteen, through the carelessness of his drunken father the family's frame home burned, killing his mother and his four sisters. George has since educated himself and his two younger brothers and has just received a special appointment from the Canadian Prime Minister. Although his father had circulated a report of his own death to cover his later misdeeds, he reappears near the end of the transcontinental train trip; he seems to accept George's efforts to reform him, but dies of a heart attack as he is preparing to participate in a train robbery. George feels disgraced and resigns his new position, but the Prime Minister refuses to accept the resignation, and Elizabeth along with many others persuades him to continue his career. However, Philip accepts George's promise that he will never ask Elizabeth to marry him.

Eventually, George and a friend visit England, where they are graciously received at the Gaddesden estate in Martindale. When Philip's health worsens, George becomes indispensable to both Philip and the pathetically dependent Mrs. Gaddesden. Before he dies, Philip asks George to marry Elizabeth and stay in England. Elizabeth insists that she will marry George only if he is true to his love of Canada. The novel closes at their model Canadian ranch house as they await the arrival of their first child.

The *Nation* commented on this novel: "The acerbity, the indignant insularity, which distinguished *Marriage à la Mode* or *Daphne* [reviewed in chapter three] are here abandoned for an almost voluptuous worship of the spirit of the new world. The machinery of adverse condition and incident is rather crude and melodramatic, and cheapens the whole performance. Otherwise the story is pleasant, emotional, feminine, characteristic of Mrs. Ward in her later and less robust mood."[34] It is not surprising that an author who consistently sought to use scenery to "explain" her heroines should have found much along the route of the Canadian Pacific to thrill her, or that she should compare some of this scenery to her beloved Westmoreland Lake Country, or that the scenery should begin the transformation of the proper English lady into a courageous colonist. But the outlines of the setting have the vagueness of a scene discovered on a once-in-a-lifetime train trip, while her description of the Gaddesden estate in England is the work of a true artist describing a familiar and beloved scene. And Mrs. Ward's patriotism is in no way compromised by her brief interest in a British colonial outpost, as is clear from her conclusion on Martindale.

And from the window, under the winter sunset, Mrs. Gaddesden could see, at right angles to her on either side, the northern and southern wings of the great house; the sloping lawns; the river winding through the park; the ivy-grown church among the trees; the distant woods and plantations; the purple outlines of the fells. Just as the room within, so the scene without was fused into a perfect harmony and keeping by the mellowing light. There was in it not a jarring note, a ragged line—age and dignity, wealth and undisputed place: Martindale expressed them all. The Gaddesdens had twice refused a peerage; and with contempt. In their belief, to be Mr. Gaddesden of Martindale was enough; a dukedom could not have bettered it.[35]

Whether or not this Gaddesden self-esteem is meant as a device to smooth the way for Elizabeth's desertion of even beautiful Martindale for marriage to a Canadian is hard to tell, but certainly one of the surprises of the novel is the ludicrous role assigned to the English gentlemen! Philip Gaddesden and Arthur Delaine are comically out of place in the wild beauty and the bigness of country that captures Elizabeth's imagination and sets off George's personality to such advantage. And while Elizabeth is basically Mrs. Ward's typical heroine, a woman of beauty, intelligence, sensitivity, and courage, George Andersen is something new. Mrs. Ward almost succeeds in creating a man who could build civilization in a wilderness, a man educated and naturally genteel but without English traditions of class. This new hero reappears in the American forester who comes to England to help Englishmen cut their timber for the war effort in *Harvest.* This fresh concept of men did not effect all her subsequent heroes; *Richard Meynell* (published in 1911; reviewed in the second chapter) has a hero almost as unrealistically flawless as Robert Elsmere (1888), and the portrait of Alec Wing, in *Eltham House* (1915) barely hints of human passions; however, both of the romances that appeared in 1913 have strong "new" touches.

VIII The Mating of Lydia, *1913*

The most striking innovation in *The Mating of Lydia* is its "gothic" setting presided over by a Scrooge-like art collector. But too many familiar "good" characters overrun the stage and the denouement is a bit insipid.

Threlfall Tower is the family home of Edmund Melrose, a man

once handsome and attractive though eccentric. Disappointed in courtship, he had turned all his energy and money to collecting art—not for sale but for possession. In Italy he had married the daughter of an expatriate English art dealer and his Italian wife. When it suited him, he brought Netta to Threlfall, expecting her to live in this strange, cold climate, in a dismal, isolated house of which only a few rooms are habitable, because he was determined to spend neither time nor money on anything but art. Netta Melrose and her Italian maid stole a valuable bronze Hermes, and taking tiny Felicia Melrose, fled to Italy. Edmund secured a divorce, settled £75 a year on his daughter, and shut his former wife out of his life. When the story begins, Threlfall Tower is served by the Dixons, an elderly couple, because they represent the economical minimum and because they do not intrude on Melrose's preoccupation with his collection. Most of the rooms are cluttered with crated art objects. There are no visitors except art agents. His land agent collects rents but is permitted no money for repairs. Melrose would just as soon the cottages fell apart and the tenants moved away. His grounds are untended.

Into this miser's lair Claude Faversham is thrust when he wrecks his bicycle at the foot of a steep hill just outside Threlfall. Dr. Undershaw insists upon moving the unconscious man to the nearest house, despite the Dixons' protests and the master's absence. When Melrose returns and attempts to evict his unwanted guests—an invalid, two nurses, and a doctor—the doctor warns Melrose that he is responsible for the invalid's life. But Faversham proves to be of interest to Melrose, especially when it is learned that the otherwise penniless young man owns the Markworth jewels, inherited from an uncle. Melrose determines to get the jewels. Faversham accepts the offer of the position of land agent, but is thwarted at every turn in his attempts to improve the deplorable conditions of the estate. Melrose then tries to "buy" the jewels with the promise that Faversham will be his heir; when Faversham refuses, Melrose starts to change his will, but is murdered. The community thinks Faversham arranged the murder to save his inheritance.

Thus far the novel is well written and something new for Mrs. Ward. But parallel with this plot runs the story of Lydia Penfold, a moderately good artist who has some ideas about the independence of women but is too pretty to offend any man for long. Her most promising suitor is Harry Tatham, master of Duddon, a beautiful and properly run neighboring estate. His widowed mother, Victoria, Lady Tatham, was once the love interest of Edmund Melrose and the one who refused his courtship. She is everything a Lady should be, and quite approves of Lydia for her sweetly normal son. Their best friend is Cyril Boden, the dedicated reformer in London slums, who comes to Duddon to recuperate when his health begins to fail. Through him Mrs. Ward preaches the themes of the book—the good and bad results of wealth, Ruskin's philosophy of art, and the Ward philosophy of religion. Friend of even Melrose's tenants, he hears the confession of one of them of the murder of Melrose and thus is able to clear Faversham. Faversham turns his inheritance over to Felicia Melrose, with the stipulation that the Tower be made a public art museum. He requests the position of first curator. Lydia feels she can marry him once he is thus cleansed of the Melrose taint of greed. Harry Tatham is consoled with the immature, ambitious Felicia, who with her mother had returned to claim what everyone but Melrose considered her rightful inheritance.

Everything at Duddon and in the Penfold cottage is normal, charming, right. Of course some order and sunshine came to Threlfall Tower when Faversham began working as agent and secretary, for together he and Melrose unpacked and arranged most of the art. And Melrose lost some of his eccentricity as he began to like Faversham, whom he really wanted as his heir. At the end, the only interesting shadow in the flooding "sweetness and light" is Melrose's daughter—blessed with the ignorance and materialism of her mother, the selfishness and intelligence of her father, she promises to stir up a storm or two in the calm lives of Harry and Victoria Tatham. While many reviewers paid the novel the usual compliments on the smoothness of Mrs. Ward's technique and the enthusiasm of her readers, the *New York Times* made the following critical comment: "Its ending is too much in accord with the conventions of romance to harmonize with the deeper social note. For, though everything did indeed 'turn out for the best,' was not that happy result due rather to the author's determined interference than to the natural course of events?"[36] What "deeper social note" the reviewer had in mind is difficult to say, since the warped point of view of the "villain," Melrose, seems to have a very localized effect. The hero is a bit less of the educated English gentleman, certainly without the usual family, position, estate and other perquisites of most of her heroes. Although slight as a literary accomplishment, it is very readable and does have considerable freshness.

IX The Coryston Family, *1913*

The Coryston Family was both praised and belittled when it appeared, in a world already turning from Victorian ideals. Yet the novel is one of the strongest Mrs. Ward wrote. The plot is of little significance except as a framework for the display of fresh examples of all the characters that populated the author's world of politics, religion, status, and romance. But each character is drawn with new individuality, and the settings and incidents are in most cases intrinsically part of the very real world of these individuals. Lady Coryston is the grand dame who sacrifices her happiness and proper place to politics. "A commanding figure! She was in black, carrying her only ornament, an embossed silver girdle and chatelaine, the gift of her husband in their first year of marriage. As she paused, motionless, in the clear sunshine, her great height and her great thinness and flatness brought out with emphasis the masculine carriage of the shoulders and the strong markings of the face. In this moment of solitude, however, the mistress of Coryston Place and of the great domain on which she looked allowed herself an expression which was scarcely that of an autocrat—"[37] Reginald Lester, the young scholar who is cataloguing the Coryston Library, serving as confidant to Arthur Coryston, and falling in love with Marcia Coryston, comments in his diary that Lady Coryston is a "full blown *tyrannus*." He speaks for the author in condemning Lady Coryston's direct interference in politics—her husband had dared to defy her and vote against her aristocratic convictions only once, just before he died; her youngest son is completely under her dominance until he falls in love with the daughter of the Chancellor, her worst political enemy; she turned her sister out, never to speak to her again, because she married a man who "ratted to the Liberals"; she is interested in a short betrothal for Marcia, because a longer one would interfere with her plans for Arthur's election; and the chief conflict of the novel is that between Lady Coryston and her eldest son, rightful heir to the power she wields but never subservient to her will and now in open rebellion against her party and practices. Lady Coryston's tyranny leads to moments of humor, and moments of pathos; and the author shows true insight when she has her surrender to her eldest son, in the end, for the same reasons that she had fought with him.

In strong contrast to the Corystons are Lord and Lady William and their son Edward Newbury, a sincerely dedicated, high-church family, who practice what they preach—to the destruction of the engagement between Edward and Marcia and the suicide of Betts, the supervisor of their model farm.

> Lord William Newbury was a man of sixty-five, tall and slenderly built. His pale hazel eyes, dreamily kind, were the prominent feature of his face; he had very thin flat cheeks, and his white hair—he was walking bareheaded—was blown back from a brow which, like the delicate mouth, was still young, almost boyish. Sweetness and a rather weak refinement—a stranger would probably have summed up his first impressions of Lord William, drawn from his bodily presence, in some such words. But the stranger who did so would have been singularly wide of the mark. His wife beside him looked even frailer and slighter than he. A small and mouse-like woman, dressed in gray clothes of the simplest and plainest make, and wearing a shady garden hat; her keen black eyes in her shriveled face gave that clear promise of strong character in which her husband's aspect, at first sight, was lacking. But Lady William knew her place. She was the most submissive and the most docile of wives; and on no other terms would life have been either possible or happy in her husband's company.[38]

Their son Edward seems the perfect blending of a piety developed through three generations of Anglo-Catholicism and the charm of the educated English gentleman. He wins Marcia in part because he is masterful, in part because he is sincerely in love with her. After their engagement is broken—because the Newburys demand that Betts either give up his job or his wife, who is a divorced woman—Edward takes orders and goes to Brindisi and Southern India. He and Marcia have a final interview, an interview "short and restrained, but not to be forgotten by either of the two."[39]

The stormy center of the Coryston-Newbury relationship is Lord Coryston, gadfly of both the Tory and the Liberal parties—sending Mrs. Betts to Marcia to tell the pathetic story of her early, unhappy marriage, her running away, her desertion and degradation, and then her redemption by marriage to Betts; or buying land and helping the Baptists build a chapel in his mother's domain. He proposes to Marian Atherstone, sensible "sounding board" for his tirades against injustice, in the same belligerent manner that he uses when describing the "politicians" of both parties. As for the Newburys! " 'Too bright and good'—aren't they?—'for human nature's daily food.' Such churches—and schools—and villages! All the little boys patterns—and all the little girls saints. Everybody singing in choirs—and belonging to confraternities—and carrying banners. 'By the pricking of my thumbs' when I see a Newbury I feel that a mere fraction divides me from the criminal class."[40] His mother's efforts to cow him fail, but he knows how to comfort her when her power and her health break, and promises to serve his country well as maturity implements his righteous indignation.

Each major character and each issue recall other novels by Mrs. Ward, yet each fits this novel and adds stature to her total work. Edward Newbury and Marcia Coryston recall the protagonists of *Helbeck of Bannisdale,* though the tragedy falls most heavily upon those unequal to the heroism required, Mr. and Mrs. Betts. Lord Coryston is a spiritual brother of Jacob Delafield, of *Lady Rose's Daughter;* Reginald Lester is kin to Claude Faversham of *The Mating of Lydia;* the excellently interpreted opera, presenting the glory of Iphegenia's decision to give herself to save her country, presents a third facet of the role of women in government and recalls the function of drama in *Miss Bretherton.*

The peripheral characters—Miss Wagstaffe or "Waggin," Marcia's retired governess; Sir Wilfrid, her godfather; Chancellor Glenwilliam and his daughter Enid, who twice refuses Arthur Coryston; James Coryston, the middle son, the aesthete who refuses to involve himself in his family's struggle, or in any struggle for that matter—these join Mrs. Ward's "Human Comedy" with a precision equal to the vital minor characters of her other novels. *The Spectator* commented: "While *The Coryston Family* exhibits all Mrs. Humphry Ward's eloquence in argument and skill in the presentation of her characters, she has come nearer to the direct portraiture of living personages than in any of her previous novels."[41] The *New York Times* clearly singles the book out as an Indian summer achievement in the author's autumn: "The whole novel is admirably balanced, a difficult achievement where there are several characters of almost equal importance. In this, as in character drawing and naturalness of plot, it is a very much better book than *The Mating of Lydia,* and one which deserves to rank with its author's best work."[42]

X Eltham House, *1915*

Eltham House is the last of her novels based, in part, on a well-known "romance." She had made her first notes in the spring of 1914, "the last spring of the Old World, when one could still listen to the thrushes singing, and watch the blooming of the gorse and the hawthorn without that tragic intervening sense which now oppresses of the veil of death and suffering. . . ."[43] The true story dates from 1796, when Lord Holland ran away with the wife of Sir Godfrey Webster, who, with difficulty, was bribed by the surrender of her fortune to divorce her. Then Lord Holland and Lady Webster were married and returned to London to "reign" for many years at Holland House. Mrs. Ward was intrigued with the idea of changing public attitudes; she wondered how the public a century later would treat such a couple. Lord Holland had suffered not at all, serving not only in the House of Lords, but in the Whig Ministries, and being received at Court without question. Proper ladies did not call on Lady Holland, but she maintained a famous salon attended exclusively by men. "So it was that the figure of Caroline Wing rose out of the mists that encircle one's first thoughts of a new subject; and in the dark days of last winter, those hours that could be spent in writing were entirely occupied in weaving the story that for months was like 'a wind-warm space' amid the horrors and griefs and tasks of the war, into which one could retreat for a little while every day and forget the newspapers."[44]

Alec and Caroline Wing return to London and open Eltham House, at the expense and insistence of Lord Wing, now seventy-four, Alec's grandfather. He wishes to give Alec everything he wants, and warns Caroline that a thwarted Alec will not be a happy lover. Soon Caroline has friends and fame as a hostess—though no respectable women will speak to her, except the Duchess, Alec's aunt. Another aunt, Lady Theodora Webb, actually keeps Caroline off a charitable committee, largely because in Lady Webb's original plans Alec was to have married her daughter. But Mrs. Washington, Nonconformist wife of the future Prime Minister, is sincerely shocked at Alec and Caroline's conduct and keeps her husband from appointing Alec to even an insignificant post. Alec turns to Madge Whitton for help in getting an unscrupulous editor for a newspaper he starts. His grandfather dies, leaving him a title and immense wealth. When he is defeated politically, he goes to South America, leaving Caroline no forwarding address. Madge finally brings him home with the news of Caroline's approaching death. But the highlight of Caroline's last weeks is the visit and affection of her child, whom her first husband has previously kept from her.

There is no way of knowing whether the original heroine, Lady Holland, was as sensitive as Caroline Wing, or the original hero, Lord Holland, as selfish as Alec Wing; so the issue of changing public attitudes is clouded by personalities. Caroline is as beautiful and emotional as Mrs. Ward's other heroines, but less intellectual. Alec is almost as "insufferable" as Manisty (*Eleanor*). The shadowy character of Caroline's first husband, John Marsworth, is the negative side of Alan Helbeck (*Helbeck of Bannisdale*) and Edward Newbury (*The Coryston Family*). Marsworth is unstable and an extremist in religious matters. After his divorce from Caroline, he enters a Jesuit order, but finds this discipline too much. He remains Catholic, but dissatisfied. The young lovers, Joyce Allen and Jim Durant, are pleasant but insignificant. The adoration Caroline receives from them and her other admirers is foreign to modern thinking; one wonders if it truly existed in the late Victorian period. The most successful character is Madge Whitton, who makes the mistake of falling in love with Alec, but who "plays the game," cynically and gallantly. Caroline's dream of a spiritualized relationship based on human sexual love was "wrong" not only by society's standards, but also according to the realistic rules of life Mrs. Ward follows in most of her novels; she was convinced that love is not enough for any man—that he must have his work and his place in the sun. What she seems to have failed to realize was that the rejection of creeds and dogma traditionally significant to both men and women would leave a void that most people would not fill with intellectual accomplishments and social service. *Eltham House* is another of her "autumn" novels, pleasant, even emotional reading, but significant only as proof that the author is consistent in style, interests and convictions.

XI A Great Success, *1916*

In the same year Mrs. Ward published two romances, *A Great Success* and *Lady Connie. Lady Connie* is her best "late" novel, but *A Great Success* can scarcely be called a novel, so slight is its plot, so undemanding its theme, a theme very close to that of Sir James Barrie's *What Every Woman Knows.*

Doris Meadows is the plain, practical young wife of brilliant but lazy Arthur Meadows, whose lectures on political celebrities have just made him one of the literary lions of the London season. Lady Dunstable takes him up and promises herself he will succeed under her patronage, and be dropped later at her pleasure. Of course Doris forms no part of Lady Dunstable's scheme. Working at her uncle's studio, earning a bit of extra money illustrating, Doris meets the Dunstables' alienated son and heir, Herbert, and an adventuress, Elena Fink, who has Herbert almost "landed." Another acquaintance furnishes background for the situation and pleads with Doris that Lord Dunstable and his neighbors do not deserve Elena Fink as a future Lady Dunstable. Doris arrives uninvited at a Scottish houseparty, to Arthur's embarrassment and Lady Dunstable's annoyance. A letter from Herbert breaks his mother's hauteur and sends his father to the rescue, while Arthur discovers that Doris, in borrowed gown and romantic setting, is really quite fascinating.

The simple domestic scenes in the Meadows home are refreshing and unique in Mrs. Ward's writing. And the portrait of Doris is the "great success" of the work. Unfortunately the description of Arthur is worse than familiar:

> He was a tall, broadly built, loose-limbed fellow, with a fine shaggy head, whereof various black locks were apt to fall forward over his eyes, needing to be constantly thrown back by a picturesque action of the hand. The features were large and regular, the complexion dark, the eyes a pale blue, under bushy brows. The whole aspect of the man, indeed was not unworthy of the adjective "Olympian," already freely applied to it by some of the enthusiastic women students attending his now famous lectures. . . . The expression of slumbrous power, the mingling of dream and energy in the Olympian countenance. . . .[45]

The novel's brevity is a virtue; the dialogue contains some wit.

The training of the heroine—"the clever daughter of a clever doctor"—reflects Mrs. Ward's contemporaneity, for Doris has had both high school and university education. There is frank recognition of the advantages of money and class and casual realistic touches, such as the frequent letter writing, an addiction of the Victorian era. Lady Dunstable is an echo of Lady Coryston, Mrs. Ward's protest to all women who prefer the political game to motherhood. Although the *Saturday Review* called it "an amusing trifle,"[46] the critics who bothered to review it recognized how obviously Mrs. Ward's lesser works outranked the best that most writers produce.

XII Lady Connie, *1916*

The best of Mrs. Ward's late novels is *Lady Connie.* As the *Boston Transcript* put it: "It was never more clear than in the pages of *Lady Connie* that Mrs. Ward holds firmly a place of her own in English fiction."[47] Imaginatively returning to the world she knew so well in the seventies and eighties, Mrs. Ward brings vividly to life for the reader the traditions and atmosphere of Oxford. More significantly, she creates young people who could fit on any university campus, and delightfully eccentric English "oldsters," who deserve to be recognized as the modern relatives of Dickens's favorites.

Lady Constance Beldlow, orphanned daughter of the Earl of Risborough, comes to Oxford to live with her maternal uncle, Ewen Hooper, a professor. Mrs. Hooper is ineffectual and jealous; one daughter, Alice, is pretty and shallow; the other daughter, Nora, is the "salt of the earth." Connie's beauty and cosmopolitan charm give her a long list of admirers, but three are important: Douglas Falloden, Greek scholar, "blood," athlete, and heir to a fortune and a title; Otto Radowitz, Polish musician, handsome, orphanned protégé of the third admirer, Alexander Sorell, ascetic professor of Greek and Latin, and once a youthful admirer of Connie's mother. Douglas and Connie are clearly destined for each other, but both are too proud to handle the "course of true love" smoothly. Her ill-advised favors to Otto lead to jealousy that spreads to group rivalry, and in a ragging incident Otto's right hand is permanently injured and his career as a pianist destroyed. Douglas' father, Sir Arthur, dies, leaving little of the reputed fortune. Bitterness and tragedy turn to understanding and spiritual maturity; and Nora and Sorell, Connie and Douglas, and Otto achieve the happiness each can rightfully lay claim to.

The novel contains the now familiar marks of Mrs. Ward's convictions—Otto, the only Catholic, has a mysterious spiritual experience that dissolves his hate for Douglas; Douglas and Connie learn through suffering; the university's theological restriction on doctoral degrees is scored. The novel is dated by reference to the giants of Mrs. Ward's youth—Pusey, Thomas Hill Green, Newman and Matthew Arnold. However, little things, such as Connie's smoking cigarettes, and the "mechanical piano" that Connie and Douglas secure for Otto, reveal the subtle changes in Mrs. Ward's fictional world, always closely allied to her real world.

The glory of the book is the perfection with which the characters are delineated, each consistent, convincing, worth knowing. Of these the most delightful are Connie's maiden aunts. Connie describes them in a letter to Nora:

"They are very nice to me, and as different as possible from each other. Aunt Marcia must have been quite good-looking and since she gave up wearing a rational dress which she patented twenty-five years ago, she has always worn either black silk or black satin, a large black satin hat, rather like the old 'pokes,' with black feathers in winter and white feathers in summer, and a variety of lace scarves—real lace—which she seems to have collected all over the world. Aunt Winifred says that the 'Unipantaloonicoat'—the name of the patented thing—lost Aunt Marcia all her lovers. They were scared by so much strength of character, and could not make up their minds to tackle her. She gave it up in order to capture the last of them—a dear old general who had adored her—but he shook his head, went off to Malta to think it out, and there died of Malta fever. She considers herself his widow and his portrait adorns her sitting-room. . . .

"Aunt Winifred is quite different. Aunt Marcia calls her a 'reactionary,' because she is very high church and great friends with all the clergy. She is a very quiet little thing, short and fair, with a long thin nose and eyes that look you through. Her two great passions are curates—especially consumptive curates—and animals. There is generally a consumptive curate living the open-air life in the garden. Mercifully the last patient has just left. As for the animals, the house is full of stray dogs and tame rabbits and squirrels that run up you and look for nuts in your pocket. There is also a mongoose, who pulled the cloth off the tea-table yesterday and ran away with all the cakes. . . ."[48]

Dickens's England lives on! And Mrs. Ward certainly was not totally deficient in humor. The whole novel reveals that recapturing of youthful freshness with the artistry of maturity that distinguishes the gifted writer.

Furthermore, the nature of the major conflict—the heroine's choice between the aesthete and the athlete—has continuing pertinence for a culture searching for a humanistic substitute for Christianity in a century in which science has eclipsed the glory and the authority of traditional religion. U. C. Knoepflmacher points out this attempt to find spiritual values in human relationships in his article "The Rival Ladies: Mrs. Humphry Ward's *Lady Connie* and D. H. Lawrence's *Lady Chatterley's Lover*."[49] Knoepflmacher makes a convincing case for Lawrence's use of plot, setting and characters from Mrs. Ward's novel. The heroines have the same first names, similar backgrounds and personalities. They must make a similar choice between men of strong physical attractiveness and men who are aesthetes. The metaphor of crippling is used in both novels. Crucial moments are related to gamekeepers. Both heroes must seek success beyond their inherited position and classical scholarship. Of course it is in the differences that the crux of the comparison lies, for Lawrence is reshaping the story to fit his philosophy—the cult of procreation, characterized by masculine virility and feminine submission. Lady Connie's "surrender" to the musician, Radowitz, is the symbolic surrender of a dance, under the influence of a mazurka. Lady Chatterley's surrender is to the writer Michaelis, but it is initiatory rather than symbolic. Her second surrender, like that of the first heroine, is to the physically dynamic mate, but Mrs. Ward's heroine stays properly within the bounds of matrimony, while Lawrence's heroine breaks these bounds to secure fulfillment. Radowitz's crippling is limited to one hand, a disablement that destroys his career as a pianist, but neither his manhood nor his talent. Chatterley's crippling takes from him his power to be the mate Lady Chatterley needs. Fallodin wins a chastened Connie, after both have been humbled and matured; Clifford loses his wife to Mellors, Lawrence's symbol of masculinity and fertility.

Knoepflmacher believes that Lawrence was indebted to such late Victorian literary figures as George Moore, Thomas Hardy, and Mrs. Ward, who felt they had a mission to fashion a morality devoid of "other-worldliness" and attuned to the "vast unexplored morality of life itself."[50] While the "late Victorian drawing-room morality which had been regarded as *avant garde* in the essays of Matthew Arnold and the novels of George Eliot," had become prosaic by 1916, Mrs. Ward dealt with sexual matters with genteel honesty. "Indeed her Arnoldian sense of 'curiosity' was praised by no less a connoisseur than . . . Henry James. . . . But like most Victorian moralists or even like James himself, she portrayed sexual love primarily as a didactic exemplum."[51] And despite the widespread misconception that Lawrence is a sensual artist, he, too, was using sex ideologically, symbolically, and didactically. For D. H. Lawrence (his self-esteem having been offended by his exclusion from genteel society because his father was a miner) could not accept Mrs. Ward's optimism with regard to either religion or Western culture; he sought, through the vitalist morality of Samuel Butler, to build an ethic that canceled the privileges of the upper class and gave their former superiority to the artist-intellectual class to which he belonged. In *Lady Chatterley's Lover*, Lawrence starts with the upper class, but he has his heroine reject the claims of class, find her initial meaning in an artist, her fulfillment in a man who embodies the ideal of masculine virility. As Knoepflmacher points out, both Mrs. Ward and Lawrence were struggling with "the void left by Victorian unbelief. For both systems are manifestations of the same nineteenth century religious humanism."[52] This comparison argues for Mrs. Ward's thematic influence, as does a similar comparison between her last novel, *Harvest*, and Lawrence's novella *The Fox* (1923), to be discussed in the next chapter.

XIII *Summary*

Contrary to the critical judgment that limits Mrs. Ward to the role of still-life painter of English country estates, a review of these twelve romances shows that her great talent was clothing the "stock" characters of romance in the appropriate details and credible responses that make the reader remember them as individuals. She does use settings effectively integrated to plot and character development, and here and there are scenes that claim the reader's attention as more than stage props, such as the Oxford countryside in which Isabel Bretherton and Eustace Kendal first become aware of the beginnings of love, or the salon over which Julie le Breton reigns, or the gothic ruins of Threlfall Tower into which Claude Faversham is carried after his bicycle accident. The first of these creates the delicate odors and pastel colors appropriate to the first-love sensations experienced by sensitive, refined persons. The second scene succeeds in creating in the reader's mind both enough detail of setting and enough insight into the artistry with which it was arranged to dramatize the brilliance and competitiveness of the society that moved up and down its elegant stairs. The third scene, with its clutter of crated art objects, its dark dusty rooms and its unkempt grounds, is more than a contrast to the properly kept estates Mrs. Ward usually pictured; Threlfall Tower is interesting in its own right.

In like manner, many of her characters play smoothly the roles assigned to them but succeed also in becoming memorable literary acquaintances. For example, Isabel Bretherton is lightly drawn in the first half of her novel, as befits her youthful beauty and inexperience; in the second half she has gained depth and stronger lines, as befits the author's argument—that a true artist must have not only beauty but trained talent. However, the strongest characterization in this novel is that of Eustace Kendal, who is, despite the title of the novel, the protagonist of the book. He it is who presents the challenge of the argument—English popular acclaim of beauty versus French appreciation of artistry. More significantly, his inner struggle—when the instincts he has buried under scholarship assert themselves and he is faced with the conflict between his belief that requires Isabel's success as the result of the training he sent her to his sister to receive and his desire that she fail and thus become willing to marry him—this struggle is close to the Jamesian requirement for realistic fiction. The painful eruption of emotion into Eustace Kendal's celibate bachelorhood is close kin to the inner drama of most of James's works.

By the time Mrs. Ward wrote *Eleanor,* the second of her "romances," sixteen years after *Miss Bretherton,* the first, cultural, religious, and political issues had become subservient to characterization, and Edward Manisty becomes an understandable—though generally unattractive—aristocrat in personality as well as social position, while Eleanor Borgoyne's deep need to love and serve, her unexpected struggle with jealousy, and her reevaluation of the meaning of her childhood faith delineate one of the most successful literary portraitures Mrs. Ward achieved.

Even Father Benecke, in the same novel, is less a vehicle of the author's argument against orthodoxy than an individual who fulfills his part in a very private drama. Again in *Lady Rose's Daughter,* Mrs. Ward creates characters whose personalities dominate the circumstances of their story. Julie le Breton's ambition and passion, and Jacob Delafield's uniqueness give both figures vitality stronger than the specific setting. In a similar manner Mrs. Ward creates memorable credibility in Lady Connie, Douglas Fallodin, William and Kitty Ashe, Lady Coryston and her eldest son, Lord Coryston.

Her secondary characters often have surprising vitality, sometimes vying successfully with the main characters for the reader's interest. Lady Henry is a worthy antagonist for Julie le Breton in *Lady Rose's Daughter;* Edward Melrose is the most effective creation of *The Mating of Lydia;* Otto Radowitz and Nora Hooper are the foils of Douglas Fallodin and Lady Connie and secondary only because they must be. The novel with the largest group of superbly drawn secondary characters is *The Coryston Family,* producing, in addition to Lady Coryston and Lord Coryston, Marcia Coryston and Edward Newbury, Arthur Coryston and Enid Glenwilliam. And Miss Wagstaffe, Lord and Lady William, and Mr. Betts, of *The Coryston Family,* might begin a long list of charming and unforgettable minor characters, such as the Countessa and the Ambassador of *Eleanor;* Lady Niton, Sir James Chide and Bobbie Forbes of *The Testing of Diana Mallory;* Aunt Marcia and Aunt Winifred, Mr. Wenlock, Master of Beaumont, Mrs. Mulholland, Alice Hooper and Mrs. Hooper of *Lady Connie.* Mrs. Ward's occasional use of banal description, such as that of Arthur Meadows in *A Great Success,* and her omission of servants and other classes of people essential to the milieu of her novels are weaknesses offset by the variety of characters presented and the ease with which each makes his entrances and exits, or rushes to meet his destiny. Even the spectrum of destiny ranges from Isabel Bretherton's success in both career and love, through Eleanor Borgoyne's spiritual victory but romantic loss and physical death, Julie le Breton's quiet appreciation of Jacob Delafield, Kitty Ashe's tortured search for emotional security, Phoebe Fenwick's uncertain return to reconciliation and nursing her husband through his final illness, the more normal happiness-after-testing of Diana Mallory, Lady Elizabeth Merton, Lydia Penfield, Doris

Meadows, Lady Connie and Marcia Coryston, to Enid Glenwilliam's determined rejection of marriage for filial duty, and Eleanor Wing's broken heart and broken body.

The stark drama of World War I was to give Mrs. Ward both new material and new heroes and heroines. And although critical opinion became weak, even negative, and her last novels reflect her waning strength, the results of the momentous events of her last years are recorded with flashes of insight, and she continues to reflect much that was characteristic of her times.

CHAPTER 5

The War: Reporting, Novels, Autobiography

ON Sunday, June 28, 1914, Archduke Franz Ferdinand and his wife, Sophie, were assassinated in the streets of Sarajevo, capital of the Austro-Hungarian province of Bosnia. On August 4, German troops rolled across the frontier into Belgium, and England was committed to the holocaust of World War I. Sarajevo had triggered a war in which eight to ten million men were to die horribly over a period of four years; the *belle époque* also died, and Europe was reborn into the modern world. Like many other Englishmen, Mrs. Ward could not believe that England and Germany and France, the most enlightened countries in the history of man, could involve themselves in such a monstrous denial of man's natural desire to improve. In her first account of the war, *England's Effort* (1916), she reports the reactions of various other English leaders. She asked a very able man in the navy, "Did you forsee it?" He replied, after some thought, "I always felt there might be a clash over some colonial question—a quarrel about black men. But a war between the white nations over a European question—that Germany would force such a war—no, that I never believed!"[1]

I *War Correspondent*

One of the world leaders who foresaw the coming horror was Theodore Roosevelt, who in 1907 promoted the Hague Peace Conference, which, however, failed to halt the arms race. When Mrs. Humphry Ward visited the United States in 1908, Theodore Roosevelt, still president, entertained her and her husband and daughter at the White House. It was on the basis of the friendship formed then that he wrote to her on December 27,

1915, from Oyster Bay, to beg her to tell America what England was doing in the war, for he was an outstanding proponent of America's participation on the side of the Allies.

My dear Mrs. Ward,

The War has been, on the whole, well presented in America from the French side. We do not think justice has been done to the English side. . . . I wish that some writer like yourself could, in a series of articles, put vividly before our people what the English people are doing. . . . What I would like our people to visualize is the effort, the resolution and the self-sacrifice of the English men and women who are determined to see this war through. . . . There is not a human being more fitted to present this matter as it should be presented than you are. I do hope you will undertake the task.

Faithfully yours,
Theodore Roosevelt

The letter reached her on January 10, 1916. She consulted such friends as Charles F. G. Masterman, Sir Gilbert Parker (Government Propaganda Department), Sir Edward Grey (Foreign Minister), Lord Robert Cecil, and Sir Arthur Nicolson. They all approved and by January 31 she had begun the adventure of being the first official woman war correspondent. David Lloyd George, then Minister of Munitions, made it possible for her to visit the principal munition-works. She made a brief visit to the fleet, lying in the Firth of Cromarty, then crossed the Straits to see the army on the field in France. The thrilling and shocking experiences of the five-week tour she translated into "Letters to an American Friend," distributed throughout America by press syndicates, then published in book form, by Scribner's, in May. Mr. Choate did the preface for the American edition, titled *England's Effort,* and published in June. Despite the pressure of producing the reports in the space of forty-five days, Mrs. Ward's style was effective and popular enough to warrant translations into several languages. Some commentators credited the book with a crucial influence on America's decision to enter the war earlier than might otherwise have been the case.

But by the end of 1916 America's entrance date was still months away and uncertain; so Mrs. Ward secured permission to make a second propaganda effort, this time based on a visit to the British Military Zone from February 18 to March 4, 1917. Then she and Dorothy journeyed on to Paris, where, under the care of

M. Ponsot, they visited the devastated areas of the Centre and the East. "Soissons, Rheims and Verdun were too dangerous, but she saw the ruins of Senlis, the battlefield of Ourcq, and other theatres of war."[3] The reports of this trip, now openly addressed to Theodore Roosevelt, appeared under the title *Towards the Goal.* The trilogy of war correspondence books was completed in 1919, when she returned to quiet battlefields "to make clear to myself if I could, and thereby to others, the true measure of the part played by the British Empire and the British Armies in the concluding campaigns of the war."[4] The result was *Fields of Victory.*

Some of the material in the three war books is still good reading—facts, figures and incidents, told with brevity and firsthand knowledge, that clearly present the Gargantuan strides England made to close the gap between her unpreparedness and her hour of destiny. Previous to this direct involvement in the war, Mrs. Ward had participated in an investigation of soldiers' pensions and efforts for reform in this area; she had helped to convert the Passmore Edwards Settlement into a temporary hostel for Belgian refugees, then to reorganize it for exclusively women's activities, since there were very few men with time for its cultural and recreational facilities. She reduced the personnel of her own establishments, and leased Stocks in the summer and Grosvenor Place during the winter. Some of these latter economies were necessitated by the war-induced reduction in her own income. Such arduous efforts, for a woman sixty-three to sixty-five, and one who had always used her frail strength to its limit, plus the personal losses among her large circle of relatives and friends, left their mark on her physically and spiritually. For a time she found some measure of tranquility and escape in the writing of the last of her nonwar fiction: *Eltham House* (1915), *A Great Success* (1916), and *Lady Connie* (1916). But after her visits to the battlefields, she dedicated her pen to the war effort and she was sustained by the united idealism of the countless men and women who were determined to make this costly conflict a "war to end wars," to destroy tyranny, and to "make the world safe for democracy."

For Mrs. Ward the most dramatic fact of the war was the great social changes it brought. She had always believed in and worked for education for women, but she had consistently opposed women's suffrage and urged women to choose marriage and motherhood above careers. Now women were filling countless "unwomanly" roles of necessity, and doing the job with more grace than she had believed possible. She had always moved among aristocrats and scholars who upheld traditions that favored gracious and aesthetic living. Now she saw common crises erase class distinctions and demand heroic activity of scholars. Janet Trevelyan writes: "To her, of course, the human interest of the scene was the all-important thing—the spectacle of the mixture of classes in the vast factories, the high-school mistresses, the parsons, the tailors' and drapers' assistants handling their machines as lovingly as the born engineers—the enormous sheds-full of women and girls of many diverse types working together with one common impulse. . . ."[5]

In her first reports, *England's Effort,* she senses the full drama involved in the struggle to persuade skilled craftsmen of arms and munitions to lay aside ancient craft restrictions and teach enough of their skills to the unskilled—both men and women—to double, triple, quadruple their output. She describes educated, refined women working among men and women of the lower classes, without friction, though such groups would never previously have considered companionship possible. She carefully answers the accusation that the wealthy and privileged were not bearing their share of the burdens by citing many instances of the sacrifice of wealth and privilege and the very high percentage of titled young men who had volunteered for military duty and had died in greater percentages than the common citizens. So, although she had been unprepared for the evil side of human nature that had produced the war, and for the decay of the social system that had nurtured her past ideals, she was sincere when she states: "There will be a new wind blowing through England when this war is done. Not only will the scientific intelligence, the general education, and the industrial plant of the nation have gained enormously from the huge impetus of war; but men and women, employers and employed, shaken perforce out of their old grooves, will look at each other surely with new eyes, in a world which has not been steeped for nothing in effort and sacrifice, in common griefs and a common passion of will."[6]

Her second book, *Towards the Goal,* was eloquently introduced by Theodore Roosevelt:

England has in this war reached a height of achievement loftier than that which she attained in the struggle with Napoleon; and she has reached that height in a far shorter period. Her giant effort, crowned with a success as wonderful as the effort itself, is worthily described by the woman who has influenced all those who speak and read English more profoundly than any other woman now alive. No other writer could describe England's effort with such knowledge, power and interest. Mrs. Ward writes nobly on a noble theme.[7]

This famous exponent of the rugged life felt that England had suffered from a "surfeit of materialism that produced a lack of spiritual purpose,"[8] but in the struggle was redeeming itself. He wanted America to cast aside its triviality and, seeing the issues in clear black and white, find glory and righteousness in the struggle. America entered the war as Mrs. Ward was writing the third letter, entitled "Easter Eve, 1917." The book is much like its predecessor, filled with facts, statistics, scenes, incidents, passionate denunciation of the cruelty and bigotry of the enemy, and praise of that tenacity of spirit that sustained the Allied Forces. Nearly all of the reviews were commendatory, for there were few objectors left in England or America by the end of 1917.

Theodore Roosevelt died January 6, 1919, so that he was saved the difficulty of reacting to Mrs. Ward's third book, *Fields of Victory,* published later that same year. For this volume she wrote the introduction, explaining her purpose. Her eagerness to retain the first rank for Britain produces a tone so condescending as to be insulting were it not quite apparent that the author is sincere and unable to see the situation differently.

We are indeed anxious and willing to share responsibilities, say in Africa and the Middle East, with America as with France. Why not? The mighty elder power is eager to see America realize her own world position, and come forward to take her share in a world-ordering, which has lain too heavy until now on England's sole shoulders. She is glad and thankful—the "weary Titan"—to hand over some of her responsibilities to America, and to share many of the rest. She wants nothing more for herself—the Great Mother of Nations—why should she? She has so much.[9]

Mrs. Ward is better remembered for her very British fiction than for her partisan journalism!

II "Missing," *1917*

The first of Mrs. Ward's war novels, *"Missing,"* dramatizes one of the most frightening realities of war—a loved one "missing, presumed dead." Nelly Cookson marries Lieutenant George Sarratt, much to the disgust of her elder sister Bridget, strong-minded, practical supervisor of the younger girl's life until this romance; for Bridget wanted Nelly's beauty to procure wealth and security for both of them. When Lieutenant Sarratt is reported missing, Bridget is joined by Sir William Farrell and his sister Cicely in encouraging Nelly to go on living. Sir William, restricted to home service by a stiff knee, falls in love with Nelly. Bridget is called to France to identify a seriously wounded, speechless soldier. Although George recognizes her, she denies her recognition of him, hoping he will die very soon and Nelly will not only be spared the knowledge of his suffering but will the sooner yield to Sir William's interest. George recovers his speech; Nelly arrives in time for his dying hours; Bridget is in disgrace. Nelly returns to England to mature through strenuous hospital service, and Sir William is given some hope, a hope approved by Nelly's visionary communion with George.

The best character portrayal is that of Bridget, whose abnormal selfishness, foolish betrayal and pathetic isolation are not reasoned away. As in the creation of Louie Grieve (*David Grieve*), Letty and Lady Tressady (*Sir George Tressady*), and Lady Henry (*Lady Rose's Daughter*), Mrs. Ward proves her knowledge of women who multiply the troubles of the world, but are their own worst enemies. The heroine, Nelly, reminds one of Fanny Price in Jane Austen's *Mansfield Park*. Such sweet dependency coupled with such tenacious love! George Sarratt is an obvious transition hero for Mrs. Ward. As the son of a Master of Harrow, and a student at Oxford on a scholarship, he is a gentleman if not an aristocrat; and of course he is the perfect English soldier, all tenderness to his young wife, but fully satisfied that war is a fine test of his manliness and his love of country. The subplot of Cicely Farrell and Captain Marsworth presents a contrasting romance, and a more realistic picture of love in the war-torn world of 1915–16.

The dialogue of the honeymooners and the description of the setting—a spot in Westmoreland strongly resembling the setting of Mrs. Ward's own honeymoon forty-five years earlier—are two of the best bits of such writing in all Mrs. Ward's novels. Understandably the war information and the mood of the novel are quite obviously based on the experiences that produced *England's Effort.* The author's super-patriotism is almost too much of a burden for her habitual techniques to sustain. But the book does hint at deeper things—the responsibility of privilege, the response of men to warfare, the essential importance of individuals over international maneuvers. More perhaps should not be expected, for few first-rate war novels have been written while a war was in progress. The novel was made into a movie, by Paramount, in 1918.

III The War and Elizabeth, *or* Elizabeth's Campaign, *1918*

The war did furnish Mrs. Ward with material different from her earlier novels; it also produced two novels that border on the new, modern technique of symbolism. The first of these symbolist novels is *The War and Elizabeth,* published in America under the title *Elizabeth's Campaign.* Although Mrs. Ward was critically aware of the work of most of her contemporaries—a brief evaluation of many of them appearing in her *A Writer's Recollections* (1918)—the symbolism she uses seems rather the result of the war than of any conscious effort on her part to imitate other writers. As the war destroyed the old genteel way of life and daily called into question the survival of traditional values, the ingredients of the emergency and the necessarily simplified social structure were invested with new and symbolic meaning. The heroine, Elizabeth Bremerton, becomes symbolic of the eternal duty of women—to provide the essentials of survival and spiritual security. The ancient trees she is determined to give to the war effort become the symbol of that part of any nation that is closest to its nature and its history—primeval nobility and faith in the renewal power of life. The Squire is symbolic of art in conflict with war. As André Malraux expresses it in *Man's Hope* (1937), when two men, one an art dealer, the other an art historian, react to the Spanish Civil War:

> "In the churches of the south where we fought, I saw the large spots of blood side by side with paintings. . . . Paintings. . .lose their force."
>
> "We need other paintings, that's all," said Alvear.

"That's placing works of art pretty high," Scali answered.
"Not works: art."
"Art is of small importance in the face of suffering and unfortunately no painting holds up in the face of spots of blood."[10]

And the Squire's barricading of the gateway to the trees and his surreptitious removal of the barricade are symbolic of his futile resistance to the war and his dark mood of surrender when Desmond is dying. "And now in the man's vain but not ignoble soul there stirred a first passing terror of what the war might do with him, if he were forced to feel it—to let it in. He saw it as a veiled Presence at the Door—and struggled with it blindly."[11]

Desmond, the "sacrificial lamb," is too beautiful, but is symbolic of the humanist ideal, a replacement of deity with deified man, and a forerunner of the "Christ-figure theme" in more recent criticism. The Victorian, humanist sentiment is expressed by Sir Henry Chicksands, who, observing a portrait of Desmond, compares him to a Greek hero: "Youth, eager, strong, self-confident, with its innocent parted lips, and its steadfast eyes looking out over the future—the drawing stood there as the quintessence, the embodiment of a whole generation. So might the young Odysseus have looked when he left his mother on his first journey. . . ."[12] Desmond's death, a sacrifice he gladly makes, is the source of redemption for his sister Pamela and the man she loves (Arthur Chicksands), for his brother Aubrey and the girl he loves (Beryl Chicksands), and for his father, who now must live with his country's great struggle.

The avenue of Mrs. Ward's journey into symbolism was her patriotism. She passionately believed in England's destiny. The sacredness of English soil she puts into Elizabeth's mouth: " 'It's perfectly monstrous!' she was thinking. 'It oughtn't to be allowed. And when we're properly civilized, it won't be allowed. No one ought to be free to ruin his land as he pleases! It concerns the State. "Manage your land decently—produce a proper amount of food—or out you go!" And I wouldn't have waited for the war to say it!' "[13] Other sentences take on symbolic meaning. "Country life is, above all, steeped in common sense—the old ancestral, simple wisdom of primitive men. And Elizabeth, in spite of her classical degree, and her passion for Greek pots, believed herself to be, before everything, a person of common sense."[14] This emphasis on the prime importance of the survival wisdom of primitive man, is given a primeval setting in the following passage:

The wood indeed, which belonged to the Squire, was a fragment of things primeval. For generations the trees in it had sprung up, flourished, and fallen as they pleased. There were corners of it where the north-west wind sweeping over the bare down above it had made pathways of death and ruin; sinister places where the fallen or broken trunks of the great beech trees, as they crashed down-hill upon and against each other, had assumed all sorts of grotesque and phantasmal attitudes, as in trampled melee of giants; there were other parts where slender, plumed trees, rising branchless to a great height above open spaces, took the shape from a distance of Italian stone palms, and gave a touch of southern or romantic grace to the English midland scene; while at their feet, the tops of the more crowded sections of the wood lay in loose, billowy masses of leaf, the oaks vividly green, the beeches already aflame.[15]

Thus this small copse mirrors the death struggles of giants, the grotesque results of their melee, the romantic spots of beauty mingled with the horror, and the touch of flame that highlights but may destroy the living green of the world.

However, the book is not all symbolism. The characters are lively, foolish, jealous, eccentric, lovable. Even Desmond makes mistakes, in the beginning, and his twin sister, Pamela, is charmingly nineteen. The Squire is stubborn, belligerent, tragic, redeemable. Elizabeth is the new woman of education and twentieth-century notions, an incurable manager, but indispensable. Aubrey is guilt ridden, a victim of war's terrifying gamble with men's lives, but a sensitive, brave man. The plot is fresh, timely, and touched with both humor and drama. Elizabeth Bremerton becomes secretary to Squire Mannering, whose son Aubrey is engaged to Beryl Chicksands. Sir Henry Chicksands is head of much patriotic effort, especially the committee charged with securing increased food production, a desperate need during Germany's submarine blockade of England. Pamela is in love with Beryl's brother, Arthur, a captain home after injuries, who thinks Pamela not yet a woman and war no time for love. Pamela persuades her twin, Desmond, that Elizabeth is a conniving woman. The Squire refuses to sacrifice his park to increase cultivation and tries to shut the war out of his consciousness. Desmond, the Squire's favorite, goes to the front, is fatally wounded, returns to Mannering to die. As Pamela brings him home, Arthur meets them and sees clearly that Pamela is a woman, the woman he loves. Aubrey confesses his bitter secret to Desmond, and cleansed of his guilt, he can now give his love fully to Beryl. And Elizabeth and the Squire come to an unspoken accord as they tenderly sort Desmond's things.

There is considerable humor in the "taming of the Squire," who is selfish, exacting, irritable, but an excellent Greek scholar and an intelligent art critic. When he rants and raves against the war, Elizabeth waits patiently, then quietly punctures his bombast. Pamela and Desmond nickname her "Broomie" in honor of the speed with which, like a new broom, she cleans up the Squire's untidy affairs. When she is forced to leave temporarily because of her mother's illness, the Squire has his own way of saying, like Henry Higgins's famous line in *Pygmalion,* "I've grown accustomed to her. . . ." His first attempt to propose is thwarted by the entrance of Captain Dell, his estate agent, who really came to see Elizabeth because he knows she is the one who is running the estate.

Once again Mrs. Ward's "religious" beliefs appear, this time praising the courage of the English soldiers. As Desmond is dying, Aubrey tells him of the incident that haunts him—he had gone for help, rested fifteen minutes, and found on his return that in the last five minutes the men (including his best friend) had all been killed. Desmond has a vision in which the deceased friend assures him, and through him Aubrey, that Aubrey was not to blame, that his failure was one of the flesh, not of the spirit. Elizabeth's prayer—for Desmond and others like him—is modern and decidedly pagan: "Forces and Powers of the Universe, be with them!—strengthen the strong, uphold the weak, comfort the dying!—for in them lies the hope of the world."[16] The usual saintly reformer wearing himself out in London's East End has been replaced with the many "saintly" people involved in the war, and the spotlight has moved from the earlier battlefields to the death struggle in France.

Mrs. Ward writes with her usual skill of the English countryside, and sympathetically portrays the struggle of antiwar sentiment in the minds of those who have a treasured way of life at stake. She tells of contemporary matters, such as girl farm laborers and new methods of agriculture and forestry, but she would not, or could not, create either the sordidness or the disillusionment of the actual battlefields. Genteel woman that she was, she could express her intellectual horror at the stupidity and cruelty of the enemy, or grasp the significance of statistics, but she could not picture *her* readers as interested in the depravity or futility that was to characterize the leading postwar fiction.

IV Cousin Philip, *or* Helena, *1919*

The third of Mrs. Ward's war novels, called *Cousin Philip* in England and *Helena* in America, bears a strong resemblance to T. S. Eliot's *Family Reunion,* a play written twenty years later. Since the latter work is by a greater writer and its structure (poetic drama modeled after Greek tragedy) is of prime importance in interpreting its theme (Orestes and the Eumenides in modern guise), comparison to the play illuminates Mrs. Ward's work, adding depth but making the story of the heroine a subplot, and consequently the American title is a misnomer, which may account for some of the adverse criticism, largely American, that the book received.

The play is set in a country estate very like the ones Mrs. Ward proved herself a master at describing, and the characters are certainly descendants of Mrs. Ward's Maxwells, Corystons, Newburys, Marshams, and Tathams. While the play's hero suffers from both inherited and personal guilt that must be expiated by spiritual quest, Mrs. Ward's hero has no inherited guilt other than the conflict arising out of inherited qualities of personality, and his expiation is found not in a journey but in the obligations of love and position—both of which Eliot's hero rejects. But other parallels of plot are striking.

Lord Buntingford, Philip Bliss, forty-four, has fallen heir to the guardianship of Helena Pitstone, nineteen, at the death of her mother, Rachel Pitstone, Philip's favorite cousin. Helena, intelligent, willful, and determined to enjoy the new freedom she has tasted as an ambulance driver, resents Philip's manner and authority. Another cousin, Cynthia Welwyn, forty-two, is their neighbor; she and Philip grew up together, and Cynthia has rejected other suitors in the hope that Philip would discover his need of her. Philip, after seven years of serious art study and a four-year marriage that ended in the death of his wife, is determined to bury his past and find his fulfillment in political service. He ignores women, although he was in his youth constantly in or out of love. Then Anna, the presumably dead wife, appears at the rectory with a son, Arthur Philip, born after she ran away from Philip, fifteen years before. The news of her death had been her means of thwarting Philip, of whom she was jealous. The son is a deaf mute, due to birth injury, and has been neglected as unteachable. He is small and frail but resembles Philip. Anna finally does die; Arthur responds to experimental therapy, which Cynthia learns to carry on because she loves this son of Philip. Helena has in the meantime replaced resentment with love, but has also gained enough maturity to leave Philip and Arthur under Cynthia's loving care. And Philip's nephew Geoffrey is ready to prove himself Helena's true mate.

The similarities between *Cousin Philip* and *Family Reunion* start with the unfortunate marriage of a British aristocrat to an unsuitable woman, abroad, without the acquaintance or influence of family or friends. In Ward's *Cousin Philip* the young husband was repulsed by episodes that disgusted his fastidious nature. "Very soon after we married, I discovered that I had ceased to love her, that there was hardly anything in common between us. And there was a woman in Paris—a married woman of my own world—cultivated, and good, and refined—who was sorry for me, who made a kind of spiritual home for me. We very nearly stepped over the edge—"[17] His guilt is the "almost" in the relationship with the other woman, and the rejection of his wife. In Eliot's *Family Reunion,* Harry, Lord Monchensey, married abroad a woman whose unsuitability seemed so to stain everything fine in him that he still feels contaminated a year after her death. Furthermore, his wish to be rid of her had grown so strong that after she was lost overboard in a storm at sea, he came to believe that he had pushed her to her death. He has traveled widely since, but his world is peopled with modern Furies that only he, his Aunt Agatha, his Cousin Mary, and his servant and chauffeur, Downing, can see. Agatha is his mother's younger sister, the woman his father really loved. When as a girl she visited her recently married older sister, Amy, Lady Monchensey, she found Lord Monchensey (Harry's father) so repulsed by his wife's personality that he was planning ways to kill her. (This situation establishes the classical continuity of sin.) Agatha kept the young husband from his foolish plans, buried her love for him under the duties of presidency of a woman's college, and secretly thought of Harry as her own son—an affectionate kinship that Harry reciprocated. Mary, daughter of a deceased cousin of Lady Monchensey, shared Harry's childhood and youth, stayed on with Lady Monchensey in the hope that Harry would return and marry her. After she partially understands what Harry is searching for, she asks Agatha to help her become a college teacher. Downing has the impeccable British servant's patient, detached attitude toward the "ghosts" that are driving Harry, and he believes that his Lordship is about to find his destiny, or whatever it is that he needs to find peace.

Thus the novel by Mrs. Ward and the play by T. S. Eliot present guilt growing out of an unsuitable marriage and crimes that were committed only in the mind. In *Cousin Philip* the hero steels himself to British reserve and patriotic duty. In *Family Reunion* the hero flees from place to place, hoping to lose his nightmares in the desert or among the city crowds. These different endings are understandable in the light of the authors' philosophies; Mrs. Ward was consistent, despite the shocks of war, in her conviction that the British aristocrat—at his best—could achieve all that life had to offer in love and service to his country; Eliot, after the cynicism of his postwar period, saw the universal need for spiritual quest. But in both works, a cousin who has known and loved the protagonist since childhood is waiting to help him; in the first she becomes his mainstay; in the second she has the satisfaction of some understanding and new courage to build a new way of life for herself. In both cases the women become teachers—Cynthia of young Arthur Philip; Mary of college girls. In a sense Cynthia is both the Agatha and the Mary of the play, for she has been Philip's counsel and friend on many occasions, and she loves him through his son, as Agatha had loved Harry's father through him. Helena, who finds herself too immature to fill Philip's need (as Mary only partially understands Harry's spiritual needs), is forced to leave, to build her life around another center, just as Mary does.

Perhaps the most striking similarity of the two works is the modern concern with compatibility in marriage as the key to the fictional conflict. And Mrs. Ward was being almost shocking for her time to suggest that one could hate his spouse, even "love" another man's wife, and still be basically a very fine person. Furthermore, she understood the conflict that educating women would introduce into the traditional patterns of marriage, although she remained an "antisuffragist" in her remedy. She has Helena's mother explain to Philip her concern for her nineteen-year-old daughter's sex life:

The only hope of happiness for a woman, she believed, lay in an honest lover, if such a lover could be found. Herself an intellectual, and a freed spirit, she had no trust in any of the new professional and technical careers into which she saw women crowding. Sex seemed to her now, as always, the dominating fact of life. . . .

She saw in her Helena the strong beginnings of sex. But she also realised the promise of intelligence, of remarkable brain development, and it seemed to her of supreme importance that sex should have the first innings in her child's life.

"If she goes to college, at once, as soon as I am gone, and her brain and her ambition are appealed to before she has time to fall in love, she will develop on that side, prematurely—marvellously—and the rest will atrophy."[18]

This frankness about sex is matched by another modern attitude, the freedom with which people thought about and talked about themselves. Helena's chaperone, Mrs. Lucy Friend, is a young widow who had previously served as a companion to an elderly woman. She is disturbed at the content and manner of Helena's first confidences.

She had lived in a world where men and women do not talk much about themselves, and as a rule instinctively avoid thinking much about themselves, as a habit tending to something they call "morbid." . . . In Helena, Lucy Friend had for the first time come across the type of which the world is now full—men and women, but especially women, who have no use any longer for the reticence of the past, who desire to know all they possibly can about themselves—their own thoughts and sensations, their own peculiarities and powers, all of which are endlessly interesting to them; and especially to the intellectually *elite* among them. Already, before the war, the younger generation which was to meet the brunt of it, was an introspective, a psychological generation. . . . Only now it is not an introspection, or a psychology which writes journals or autobiography. It is the introspection which *talks*: a psychology which chatters, of all things small and great; asking its Socratic way, through all the questions of the moment, the most trivial, and the most tremendous.[19]

This concern with sex and with discussing one's self are accurate prophecies of the dominant themes of modern literature. Her contemporaries that wrote of these themes without her propriety—Thomas Hardy and D. H. Lawrence, to name two—were rejected until the reading public should recognize its own changing interests, but she continued to be read, and in the framework of acceptable social mores was truer to life than those who pictured "shocking" extremes.

V Harvest, *1920*

Mrs. Ward's last book, *Harvest,* is the second of her novels written in a symbolist mode. The title is of course symbolic of the goal of agricultural labor, and in its specific setting, of the military victory for which so many had labored for four years. The harvest in changed patterns of life was yet to be reckoned when Mrs. Ward wrote her novel. The personal harvest of the heroine is that mixture of good and evil that was beginning to puzzle the world at the end of a war that destroyed much, but gave ideals, progress and hope to many. The symbolism of the cycles of life are represented in the farm's legendary ghost and the living ghost—Rachel's former husband. One of the specific symbols is the structure of the main room of the farm house, a room with windows at both ends so that one could see inside from either end, or all the way through the house. This surrealistic visibility of things beyond the first level of insight is used as a plot device leading to Rachel's murder in the end, but is also symbolic of the new understanding of herself she must achieve before she can be worthy of George's love. In the first chapter Rachel drops an object out of her past into the well, assuring herself that the act symbolizes the end of the past. Here the symbolism may well point to the contamination of the present with the poison of the past sin, or, in reverse, the purification of the past with the deep waters of the spirit. In her diary confession before George arrives to reassure her of his love, Rachel writes: "In the Gospel, it was the bad women who were forgiven because they loved 'much.' Now I understand why. Because love makes new. It is so terribly strong. It is either a poison—or—life—immortal life."[20]

The plot is a simple one. Rachel Henderson leases the Great End farm near Ipscombe to lead an independent life as a woman farmer, with the companionship of her friend Janet Leighton, who will have charge of the dairy work. The neighboring woods have been commandeered by the government and are being cut with Canadian crews under the supervision of a New Englander, George Ellesborough. Janet is thirty-two, plain and spiritual; Rachel is twenty-seven, beautiful, and alternately sensitive and hard. They met taking agricultural training at college. Rachel's Canadian past—an early marriage to an English cad, the death of her baby, three days spent with a sympathetic male neighbor—returns to ruin her newfound happiness in engagement to George. With Janet's help Rachel achieves the courage to tell everything to George; but just as he takes her in his arms, her crazed ex-husband shoots her, fatally.

One of the strengths of the novel is the naturalness of the dialogue and the actions, in that "new" England Mrs. Ward saw growing out of the war. There is not a single aristocrat to cast a shadow across the importance of working men and women, some with college educations and small inheritances, but all dependent upon their native initiative. Furthermore, George Ellesborough is a lightly drawn but convincing American. The most demanding characterization is that of Roger Delane, Rachel's husband, in his relations to Rachel, to his sister, to his second wife, to his child; and again Mrs. Ward has succeeded significantly in the delineation of an abnormal personality.

Harvest was written by an author no longer passionately involved in her characters and their intellectual concepts, but by an author still interested in her changing world and in human beings. The steady though perceptibly weaker pace of this last work from the heart and hand of a writer now sixty-eight years old drew unfavorable reviews. "Mrs. Ward cannot be judged by *Harvest.* It is a plain mystery novel; it bears the impress of her desire to emerge from the library and to walk in the cornfields—in the new land which is war-time England. But she is unhappy in such surroundings and her serenity is gone."[21] No doubt had she been as "serene" as in earlier novels some critics would have objected to her insensitivity to the world-shaking events that surrounded her. For the contradictions in critical comment that she had herself noted early in her career, continued to the end. While Dorothy Scarborough wrote bitingly in *Bookman* that "the present book [*Cousin Philip*] is written with the top of her mind, without inside help from the heart. The author may simply have turned her well-trained typewriter loose with it while she went on a needed vacation,"[22] the London *Times* commented: "A grasp of social values has always been one of Mrs. Ward's assets as a novelist; and she employs it here to remind or inform her readers that restlessness, contempt for authority, and impatience of convention are not entirely the product of the war."[23] Of *"Missing"* the *Dial* wrote, "*'Missing'* might be a contribution to the contemporary literature about women, as vital in its way as *A Woman of Genius,* but, like most of Mrs. Ward's work, it lacks reality. It is cleverly staged, self-managed drama of the Pinero Type."[24] But the *Boston Transcript*'s E.F.E. said of the same novel: "If the war must enter fiction, it can scarcely enter it more wisely and more significantly than in Mrs. Ward's latest novel."[25] Of *The War and Elizabeth* the *Nation* commented: "The story has Mrs. Ward's old fluency, but is too clearly contrived, and too slender in characterization, to be impressive."[26] But *Outlook* concluded that "Mrs. Ward has never been more successful in rendering character and in presenting English social life in its actuality."[27]

That all of her last works should be dismissed as second rate, by some critics, is not surprising, since her very consistency bored many, and no writer of twenty-five major works of fiction can fail to produce his own unfavorable critical comparisons. However, time often makes telling comment on works of art in ways contemporary critics cannot foresee. Three years after the appearance of Mrs. Ward's last novel, *Harvest,* D. H. Lawrence's novella *The Fox* was published, in 1923, revealing similarities too numerous to be coincidental. Both stories have two young English women running a farm during the closing years of the war. One young woman in each case is physically stronger than the other and assumes the role of male leadership in the farm work; the weaker of the two, in each story, wears glasses. In both stories the farm is isolated, is near a wood from which comes danger, and the cutting of timber, under wartime regulations, is significant to the outcome of the story. Both heroes have spent the years immediately preceding the story in Canada; both respond promptly and forcefully to a letter from the heroine putting obstacles in the path of their planned marriages. Both heroines are moody; both have beautiful big eyes and feminine softness that belie their frequent appearance in semimasculine garb. Both authors resolve their respective conflicts with the death of one of the young women—but Mrs. Ward kills her romantic heroine, Rachel Henderson, while Lawrence kills the nonromantic companion, Jill Banford.

But it is in the differences between the two works that the evidence most clearly suggests that Lawrence was retelling Mrs. Ward's story. Mrs. Ward's novel carries, as usual, authentic detail of current social significance—university training of women, in this case specifically designed to fill the manpower gap produced by the war; England's desperate need for increased agricultural productivity because of the German blockade; the mixed feelings of the common people concerning the terrible loss in young life but the unprecedented wages and recognition of individual worth. But she is primarily concerned with an evaluation of the new attitudes toward sex. While her American hero is made convincingly romantic or Victorian about sex and marriage by his New England background, she depicts her heroine as being aware of the new sex codes that argued "the indelible traces and effects of an act of weakness or passion that the sentimental and goody-goody people talk of, in the majority of cases. . .don't exist."[28] Furthermore, Mrs. Ward had both Janet and George completely forgive Rachel for her lapse from chastity—the three nights spent with Dick Tanner. And she has Rachel killed, not by any trustworthy representative of society or its laws, but by a man who himself has broken most of society's codes and verges on insanity. The portrait of Rachel exploits her attractiveness to all men and her conscious manipulation of this endowment. And as the romance between her and George crests, "the male looked out upon her, kindling—by the old, old law—the woman in her."[29] But Mrs. Ward presents in George the proper balance, as she saw it, between male dominance and the new woman. He feels "a deep admiration for and sympathy with her honourable independence, for these new powers in women that made them so strong in spite of their weakness." He heartily approves of her heroic wartime competence, but his "natural instinct hungered to take her in his arms, to work for her, to put her back in the shelter of love and home. . . ."[30]

Lawrence is best known for his substitution of the principle of human sexual union for what he considered the defunct dogma of Christianity. His statement of the necessary male dominance and female submission is the burden of the last six pages of *The Fox*. "She had to be passive, to acquiesce, and to be submerged under the surface of love. . .to be like the seaweed she saw as she peered down from the boat, swaying for ever delicately under water. . . ."[31] Nellie March fights her surrender, because she has for several years filled the male role on the Bailey farm; but Henry Grenfel, now her husband, is sure that eventually she will relax and give in to him. "Then he would have all his own life as a young man and a male, and she would have all her own life as a woman and a female."[32]

Because he disagreed with Mrs. Ward's partial acceptance of the "new" independence in women, Lawrence approved of Roger Delane's possessiveness rather than George Ellesborough's admiration and generous tenderness. To prove his position, Lawrence combines Mrs. Ward's hero and her villain, and adds the animal symbol of the fox to strengthen his contention that his philosophy is the natural one. Thus in *Harvest,* Roger, the villain, had been married to Rachel, in Canada; he now frequents the woods near Rachel and Janet's farm, sneaking in and out, chiefly at night; exacts tribute of the farm's productivity; meets Rachel in a lonely spot and frightens her into a semiconscious state; disturbs her sleep and her daytime thoughts; kills her and himself. George, the hero, takes two meetings to propose, plans marriage around the demands of his military commitment, cycles from his camp to the farm, hopes to establish his new home in America. In *The Fox,* the fox sneaks in and out of the woods near March (Lawrence uses the less personal surname rather than the first name, perhaps because the women are, from the male viewpoint, types of the female of the species rather than individual personalities) and Banford's farm, chiefly at night, exacts tribute of the farm's products, meets March in a lonely spot and casts a spell over her, and dominates her dreams and her daytime moods. Henry resembles the fox, takes over the fox's dominance of March, kills the fox, uses two occasions to secure March's consent to marriage, plans the marriage around his military schedule, cycles from his encampment to the farm, kills Banford, marries March, and counts on their establishment in Canada to bring about her complete surrender.

Further, Roger had been a disappointment to his family; Henry had been a disappointment to his grandfather. George had developed his knowledge of the lumber business in Canada before the war, a knowledge that placed him in charge of

Canadians cutting English timber near Rachel and Janet's farm. Henry had learned his skill with an axe in Canada, before the war, a skill that enabled him to "innocently" kill Banford with the felled tree. Both George and Henry are experiencing love for the first time. And in Henry's final plans the movement of the theme—the male-female relationship—is reversed or returned to its original situation: marriage, in Canada, of a beautiful and moody woman to a man who is governed by his masculine need to possess the woman he passionately desires. Mrs. Ward's progressive enlightenment has been replaced with primal instincts.

Whether or not Lawrence meant to imply that the relationship between his two women was a Lesbian one—an interpretation that supports his contention that only the male-female relationship he outlines is a satisfactory one—he does change Mrs. Ward's situation in a manner that makes such a sexual relationship possible. Although there are two bedrooms in both farmhouses, while Mrs. Ward has Rachel decide which will be Janet's and which her own in the first chapter of *Harvest*, Lawrence has the two women in *The Fox* forced to sleep together by the presence of Banford's grandfather during their first year on the farm. This arrangement is continued after the grandfather's death, making it possible upon Henry's arrival for him to sleep in the "spare" bedroom. And while both authors describe the friendship between the women as having much true affection in it, Mrs. Ward's physically weaker woman is spiritually the stronger and assists the romance of her friend in every way possible. Lawrence's companion woman, like her parents, is spiritually petty; and she becomes possessive—female possessiveness is the cardinal sin for Lawrence—and does all in her power to prevent the marriage of her friend.

There are other differences reflecting Lawrence's rejection of much that Mrs. Ward's novels stand for. Mrs. Ward's heroine had inherited three thousand pounds from an opportunely deceased uncle; Lawrence's heroine was penniless, and the money was furnished by Banford's parents, who are grimly present at their daughter's accidental death. Mrs. Ward's farm adventure is a success; Lawrence's experiment in female independence must, of course, be a failure. Mrs. Ward's women had met at university classes; Lawrence's heroine had learned carpentry and joinery at evening classes, and the beginning of her friendship with

Banford is never explained. Although Mrs. Ward's characters are of a social class lower than that she usually wrote about, they are genteel and educated beyond the level of the laboring class, and they clearly represent her conviction that change will be chiefly progress. Lawrence deals with a class lower on the social scale, a class whose gentility is more protested than apparent. Mrs. Ward carefully relates her plot to war events; Lawrence is vague about the passing of time and his characters' relation to this international situation—their absorption with their own concerns is appropriate to their limited intellectual horizons. A similar contrast between the patriotic involvement of the educated and the uneducated classes is reflected in the setting and cast of characters: Mrs. Ward presents a broad, detailed setting and a large cast; Lawrence concentrates on a limited setting and a cast of five human beings and a fox.

The widespread popularity of Mrs. Ward's novels, Lawrence's passionate disagreement with the mores of his day, and the striking similarities and differences in the two works just discussed would appear to be trustworthy evidence that Lawrence had read Mrs. Ward's novel *Harvest* shortly after it appeared and set forth his refutation of her philosophy in *The Fox.* Mrs. Ward did not live to comment on this use of her material, nor did she live to finish the autobiography that many had hoped for; her *A Writer's Recollections,* appearing in 1918, brings her memoirs only to 1900.

VI A Writer's Recollections, *1918*

The arrival in England from Tasmania of the vivacious five-year-old Mary Augusta Arnold, and the spiritual saga of Thomas Arnold, her father, begin *A Writer's Recollections.* In semi-chronological order the work traces the lives of her famous relatives and friends, the development of her specific novels, and the working out of her social reform projects. Vignettes of famous people and critical comments on contemporary writers are the work's major contribution. Descriptions of her father, her uncle (Matthew Arnold) and the other members of the talented Arnold family, of Arthur Stanley, Charlotte Brontë, Arthur Hugh Clough, Doctor Newman, Benjamin Jowett, Mark Pattison, George Eliot, Thomas Hill Green, Walter Pater, and a long list of other men and women who were a part of those early years when she was not yet a celebrity in her own right make excellent reading. Recounting the events after 1888, the year *Robert Elsmere* appeared, her style takes on the tones of both critic and defender of principles. However, she is always the gracious lady, whose standards of good taste excluded any of the self-revelation or intimate comment on family or acquaintances that is so familiar in modern writing. Never is she betrayed into indiscretion, and only once into sharpness—in commenting on Lytton Strachey's "foolish essay" on her grandfather:

At the moment of correcting these proofs, my attention has been called to a foolish essay on my grandfather by Mr. Lytton Strachey, none the less foolish because it is the work of an extremely clever man. If Mr. Strachey imagines that the effect of my grandfather's life and character upon men like Stanley and Clough, or a score of others who could be named, can be accounted for by the eidolon he presents to his readers in place of the real human being, one can only regard it as one proof the more of the ease with which a certain kind of ability outsits itself.[33]

More characteristic of the combination of critic and creator that marks everything Mrs. Ward wrote is the passage on Mary Ann Evans.

She recalls a kind tête-à-tête with George Eliot, at the home of the Mark Pattisons, when she was yet a shy girl in her teens. She had been disappointed at the dinner that Miss Eliot had permitted George Lewes to do all the talking; however, when the rest of the party left the drawing room to smoke in the gallery, George Eliot asked Mary Arnold if she would like to hear about the recent Spanish Journey made by the author in preparation for *The Spanish Gypsy.*

George Eliot sat down in the darkness, and I beside her. Then she talked for about twenty minutes, with perfect ease and finish, without misplacing a word or dropping a sentence, and I realized at last that I was in the presence of a great writer. Not a great *talker*. It is clear that George Eliot never was that. Impossible for her to "talk" her books, or evolve her books from conversation, like Madame de Staël. She was too self-conscious, too desperately reflective, too rich in second-thoughts for that. But in tête-à-tête, and with time to choose her words she could—in monologue, with just enough stimulus from a companion to keep it going—produce on a listener exactly the impression of some of her best work. As the low, clear voice flowed on in Mrs. Pattison's drawing-room, I *saw* Saragossa, Granada, the Escorial, and that survival of the old Europe in the new, which one must go to Spain to find. Not that the description was particularly vivid—in talking of famous places John Richard Green could make words tell and paint with far greater success; but it was singularly complete and accomplished. When it was done the effect was there—the effect she had meant to produce. I shut my eyes, and it all comes back—the darkened room, the long, pallid face, set in black lace, the evident wish to be kind to a young girl.[34]

Mrs. Ward's fullest comments on a contemporary were devoted to Henry James, whose friendship and appreciative criticism she rightly valued. The seventh chapter of her *Recollections* is entitled "The Villa Barberini. Henry James." She praises his knowledge of the arts and humanities, his gracious manners with high and low. She labels him a "super-subtle, supersensitive cosmopolitan," but frankly contrasts his conversation and his writing.

He was politely certain, to begin with, that you knew it all; then to walk *with you* round and round the subject, turning it inside out, playing with it, making mock of it, and catching it again with a sudden grip, or a momentary flash of eloquence, seemed to be for the moment his business in life. How the thing emerged, after a few minutes, from the long involved sentences!—only involved because the impressions of a man of genius are so many, and the resources of speech so limited. This involution, this deliberation in attack, this slowness of approach toward a point which in the end was generally triumphantly rushed, always seemed to me more effective as Mr. James used it in speech than as he employed it—some of us would say, to excess—in a few of his latest books. For, in talk, his own living personality—his flashes of fun—of courtesy—of "chaff"—were always there, to do away with what, in the written word, became a difficult strain on attention.[35]

Much of her purely critical comment is given in the Epilogue, in which she touches on Tennyson, Stevenson, Hardy, Kipling, Barrie, Shaw, Wells, Conrad, Galsworthy, and a number of French writers. For most she has praise and identifies some facet of their abilities. Her judgments are naturally colored by her strong convictions, especially her religious beliefs. For example, she assures the reader of the lasting quality of Tennyson's lyrical creations but discounts his religious insights. She recognizes that the fame of the poet laureate had begun to wane during his last years, but she felt his work was due for a revival of critical interest.

What was merely didactic in Tennyson is dead years ago; the difficulties of faith and philosophy, with which his own mind had wrestled, were, long before his death, swallowed up in others far more vital, to which his various optimisms, for all the grace in which he clothed them, had no key, or suggestion of a key, to offer. The "Idylls" so popular in their day, and almost all, indeed, of the narrative and dramatic work, no longer answer to the needs of a generation that has learned from younger singers and thinkers a more restless method, a more poignant and discontented thought. A literary world fed on Meredith and Henry James, on Ibsen or Bernard Shaw or Anatole France, or Synge or Yeats, rebels against the versified argument, however musical or skilful, built up in "In Memoriam," and makes mock of what it conceives to be the false history and weak sentiment of the "Idylls." . . . It may be that one small volume will ultimately contain all that is really immortal in Tennyson's work.[36]

The revival of critical interest in Tennyson did begin shortly after Mrs. Ward's writing of these comments, with Sir Harold Nicolson's *Tennyson: Aspects of His Life, Character and Poetry,* in 1923. And many of the critical approaches in the ensuing four decades attempted to find that "small volume" of immortal poetry—by fragmentation or selection to fit philosophical and religious viewpoints ranging from that of Mrs. Ward to the conversion or growth pattern of Jerome Hamilton Buckley's *Tennyson: The Growth of a Poet,* published in 1960. The more recent critical approach to his total work, in such studies as Elton Edward Smith's *The Two Voices: A Tennyson Study* (1964), reveal the poet as a consistently modern man with unresolved tensions of doubt and faith, sense and soul, art and society.

Mrs. Ward confesses herself a late discoverer of Thomas Hardy.

How intimately have the scenes and characters of Mr. Hardy's books entered into the mind and memory of his country, compelling many persons, slowly and by degrees—I count myself among this tardy company—to realize their truth, sincerity, and humanity, in spite of the pessimism with which so many of them are tinged; their beauty also, notwithstanding the clashing discords that a poet, who is also a realist, cannot fail to strike; their permanence in English literature; and the greatness of Mr. Hardy's genius! Personally, I would make only one exception. I wish Mr. Hardy had not written *Jude the Obscure*![37]

She does not explain her disapprobation of this one work.

Perhaps for one whose novels handle similar subjects with a restraint more acceptable to her readers than Hardy's frankness—the furor raised by *Jude* turned Hardy from novel writing back to poetry—no explanation seemed necessary. And a final selection shows that when she permitted herself to be wholly critical, her metaphor and diction acquired a refreshing raciness.

> Mr. Wells seems to me a journalist of very great powers, of unequal education, and much crudity of mind, who has inadvertently strayed into the literature of imagination. The earlier books were excellent story-telling, though without any Stevensonian distinction; *Kipps* was almost a masterpiece; *Tono-Bungay* a piece of admirable fooling, enriched with some real character-creation, a thing extremely rare in Mr. Wells's books; while *Mr. Britling Sees It Through* is perhaps more likely to live than any of his novels, because the subject with which it deals comes home so closely to so vast an audience. Mr. Britling, considered as a character, has neither life nor joints. He, like the many other heroes from other Wells novels, whose names one can never recollect, is Mr. Wells himself, talking this time on a supremely interesting topic, and often talking extraordinarily well.[38]

A Writer's Recollections is disappointing autobiography but an accurate reflection of Edwardian England seen through the eyes of an intelligent, articulate, popular writer, a woman who insisted on her right both to intellectual opinions and to feminine interests, an author who absorbed impressions of her world and successfully clothed them in fiction.

CHAPTER 6

Conclusion

IN 1967, Mrs. Humphry Ward's best-known novel, *Robert Elsmere,* was published in paperback; *A Writer's Recollections* was reprinted in 1973 and 1974; and *Helbeck of Bannisdale* was reprinted in 1975. In 1973 a new biography of Mrs. Ward appeared;[1] in 1976, a book-length study of her religious views was published.[2] Whether or not these publications signal a scholarly or popular rediscovery of this famous Victorian remains to be seen. But two significant questions can be answered with some accuracy: to what extent did she reflect her world, and how much artistic merit do her best works have? A review of critical comment from both her contemporaries and more modern critics may serve as a background for the conclusions drawn by this study.

J. Stuart Walters, in his biography *Mrs. Humphry Ward, Her Work and Influence,* published in London in 1912, relates the cultural, social, political, and religious thought of the mid-nineteenth century (her inheritance), and of the half-century preceding his writing (her milieu) to her literary and civic accomplishments. He points out that "all the Arnolds worshipped Culture, and she appears to have been no exception, though it must be observed that in her later work there is evidence of a broadening of the mind on this point. . . ."[3] He discusses at length the special influences of her uncle Matthew Arnold, classifying her major characters by Arnold's famous classifications: Barbarians, Philistines, Populace, Cultured; counting her references to Arnold-approved writers; and citing diction, incidents, and other evidences of French influences in accord with Arnold's Francophile standards. He even finds evidence that Matthew Arnold's prejudice against sectarian or dissenting religious groups is repeated in her novels. His evidence that she spoke for her age is convincing. In 1912 many critics would have agreed with his estimate: "There are few literary personalities, if indeed there be any, that have made a deeper impression on the psychosis of our own times than that of Mary August . . .Arnold."[4]

However, by her death in 1920, the critical chorus was modulated with judicious praise of her near-greatness and an occasional note of discordant condemnation, by those weary of all things Victorian or of Mrs. Ward in particular. In April 1920 Muriel Harris wrote eulogistically, for the *Nation*, "The death of Mrs. Humphry Ward represents not only the end of a manifold career, but the end of an epoch. There is no one to fill her place in English society, because there is no one left with the early Victorian idea of modern greatness."[5] In June the same critic wrote an article for the *North American Review*, commenting that "if propaganda had been a fine art in Mrs. Ward's youth, she would have been among the most distinguished propagandists."[6] Harris places Mrs. Ward in the stream of great women writers of romance and concludes that, although her novels seemed artificial to many people because of their double motive, she carried conviction to the multitude because she so obviously believed her own "propaganda."

One of the discordant voices was that of William Lyon Phelps, whose collection of *Essays on Modern Novelists* was written over a period of years but appeared in book form after Mrs. Ward's death, in 1921. In the tenth chapter, entitled "Mrs. Humphry Ward," he exclaims vehemently: "It is high time that somebody spoke out his mind about Mrs. Humphry Ward. Her prodigious vogue is one of the most extraordinary literary phenomena of our day. A roar of approval greets the publication of every new novel from her active pen, and it is almost pathetic to contemplate the reverent awe of her army of worshippers when they behold the solemn announcement that she is 'collecting material' for another masterpiece."[7] Phelps finds all her studious, intellectual heroes dusty and witless. Unfortunately he carelessly confuses heroes and villains, heroines and villainesses, and finds no one but the old men effective characterizations. He concedes that she is never vulgar, sensational, or cheap, but finds her completely without humor or charm. He classes *Bessie Costrell* as her only positively bad book, and rates *David Grieve* as the only book that is almost a novel.

Lionel Stevenson, writing in 1960, agrees in part with Phelps. "Mrs. Ward was deficient not only in humor but in a novelist's essential gift of being able to create living characters. Her people are seldom more than dummy figures to express conflicting opinions. Nevertheless, she captured the mood of her decade so completely and her books were so solidly constructed and so tolerantly reasonable that Tolstoi was not alone in declaring her to be the greatest living English novelist."[8]

Both Phelps and Stevenson concede her popularity and her basic writing skills; their attack on her characterization is not echoed by those closer to the "reality" she sought to portray. In 1903 Harriet Preston had written of *Lady Rose's Daughter:* "The group of highly distinguished Englishmen who frequent the drawing-room in Bruton Street,—cabinet ministers, famous generals, diplomatists in their sixties and seventies who have given check to the stealthy moves of Russia or the Afghan frontier, or known Byron and Shelley and 'seen Harriet,'—all these are beautifully drawn and discriminated by Mrs. Ward."[9] And in 1905 C. H. Gaines wrote: "Never was the advantage of Mrs. Ward's method of composition more fully demonstrated than in *The Marriage of William Ashe.* The crisis is balanced with absolute nicety; the weight of a hair will turn the scales. The minor characters of Mrs. Ward's story are drawn with subtlety and power. All in all, *The Marriage of William Ashe* is to be regarded as an achievement of consummate art."[10] Even the American dean of Realism, William Dean Howells, devoted a chapter to Mrs. Ward in his *Heroines of Fiction* (1901), on the merits of her novel *Eleanor.*

> Her manner is still marked by the ejaculatory and suspiratory self-indulgence of the minor English novelists, to which George Eliot herself was not superior. She draws her breath in open pathos, and she caresses a situation or a character with a pitying epithet or adjective, as George Eliot does in the case of some heroine she likes very much, notably Maggie Tulliver, or Janet Dempster, and less notably Dorothea Brooke. The foible is characteristic of all but the finest artists in English fiction, and in her greater moments Mrs. Ward does not indulge it.[11]

Enid Huws Jones, in her excellent biography *Mrs. Humphry Ward* (1973)—which had access to letters, diaries, and other material not previously available—finds evidence that Mrs. Ward was aware of her decline in popularity as early as 1907. Nevertheless, Jones comments that in her second novel of 1913, *The Coryston Family,* she produced "one of her most powerful portraits of a rich old female tyrant, 'a Lady Macbeth of the drawing-room.' " Furthermore, Mrs. Ward was still determinedly current, including in her work motor-cars, ladies smoking, a lover who seeks to kiss the lips of the heroine, and good estate management practices according to the Agricultural Workers' Union.[12] Jones concludes:

> It is the content and values of her novels which are now interesting. In 1953 Miss Violet Markham, an octogenarian whose respect for Mrs. Humphry Ward had never faltered even after she herself had left the anti-suffrage movement, spoke up for the novels in a letter to *The Times*—"I am rash enough to prophesy that within another fifty years Mrs. Humphry Ward will know a come-back. Students yet unborn may well turn to the social types she sketched with so much skill as documentary evidence of a vanished age of wealth, culture and leisure."[13]

In addition to this "documentary" value, another modern critic, William S. Peterson, in his *Victorian Heretic: Mrs. Humphry Ward's Robert Elsmere* (1976), finds the artistic quality of intensity in all her religious novels except the last, *The Case of Richard Meynell.* He bases his interpretation on an analysis of Mrs. Ward's own personal struggles with the conflict between orthodoxy and enlightenment. And he points out the irony in her declining popularity by showing that by ordinary standards even *Richard Meynell* was a widely read and reviewed book, but that by comparison with the much greater success of her earlier books, it was a "failure," especially in the light of her financial needs. He concludes that there is no fault in her knowledge of the literature of Modernism, only in her awareness of cultural changes:

> Where she went astray was not in her scholarship, which was impeccable, but in her reading of the temper of the new century, for Mrs. Ward's Victorian sensibility misled her into believing that the majority of men and women were hungering and thirsting for a modernized version of Christianity. She had not taken sufficiently into account the growing secularization of the contemporary world, the decline of all institutional forms of Christianity, whether conservative or liberal, and the widespread indifference to theological questions. The fallacy of *The Case of Richard Meynell* was Mrs. Ward's assumption that most of her readers shared her own deep-seated

desire to return once again to the Communion rail of the Church in order to recover an elusive peace of mind.[14]

There are some who would consider Peterson premature in announcing the demise of institutional religion and many who would characterize the present era as a frantic search of thousands for that "elusive peace of mind." However, insofar as Mrs. Ward's books sought to educate her day on various issues—from liberalizing the national church to protesting women's suffrage—they are out of date. Insofar as she portrayed the drama and significance of the relationships of men and women, individuals and institutions, traditions and changes, she produced novels worth the continued interest of critics, scholars, and readers.

The quantity of her work and her commitment to popularity may have cost her literary stature, but a careful, unbiased reading of her novels and a study of her times lead to the conclusion that she portrayed her segment of Victorian-Edwardian England with remarkable accuracy. She knew the artistic, intellectual, and political life of England with that special insight that comes to those who earn their right to belong to these classes. And to the good fortune of innate talent and excellent family connections she added the rigorous self-discipline of scholarship and social status. Her life and work reveal that she understood the essence of Victorian England—a passionate urge to make the world better without losing control of the complex and powerful forces that made such progress possible. One means of that control was, for Mrs. Ward and her many readers, the social structure she portrayed as furnishing the ideals and traditions, the talents and leisure this reforming effort required.

Artistically, she succeeds more frequently than most writers in effectively blending setting, character, and plot. Her awareness of tradition joined to her somewhat mystical response to much of the English countryside achieved a distillation of time and place that subtly influences not only the story but the reader. Such moments range in mood from Catherine Elsmere's striding across her rugged native hills on an errand of mercy, to the foreboding disintegration of Bannisdale that surrounds Laura Fountain's suicide. They range in intensity from Robert Elsmere's cry of apostasy to the sputtering protests of the Squire in *The War and*

Elizabeth. They range in characterization from the abnormal Louie Grieve to the refreshing naturalness of Lady Niton in *The Testing of Diana Mallory.* And Mrs. Ward's subtle but sincere sympathy for all of the many and varied characters she created gives her a measure of artistry worthy of continued recognition.

Notes and References

Chapter One

1. Janet Penrose Trevelyan, *The Life of Mrs. Humphry Ward* (New York, 1923), p. 55.
2. *A Writer's Recollections* (New York, 1918), I, 8.
3. Enid Huws Jones, *Mrs. Humphry Ward* (New York, 1973), p. 15.
4. Trevelyan, p. 12.
5. Ibid., p. 27.

Chapter Two

1. *The Journal Intime of Henri Frederic Amiel,* translation, introduction, and notes by Mrs. Humphry Ward (New York, 1928), p. l [small Roman numeral for 50].
2. Ibid., p. liv.
3. Ibid.
4. Ibid., pp. liv–lv.
5. Trevelyan, p. 32.
6. *Robert Elsmere,* Chapter XXVI.
7. Ibid., Chapter XXV.
8. Ibid., Chapter XXVI.
9. Ibid.
10. Ibid., Chapter XXXII.
11. Ibid., Chapter XLI.
12. William E. Gladstone, "*Robert Elsmere* and the Battle of Belief," *Nineteenth Century* XXIII (May 1888): 766–88.
13. "The New Reformation, a Dialogue," *Nineteenth Century* XXIII (January 1889): 454–80.
14. "*Robert Elsmere,*" *Quarterly Review* CLXVII (October 1888): 276.
15. Ibid., p. 275.
16. Trevelyan, p. 51.
17. Clyde DeL. Ryals, "Introduction," Mrs. Humphry Ward, *Robert Elsmere* (Lincoln, Nebraska, 1967), p. xxx.
18. William S. Peterson, *Victorian Heretic: Mrs. Humphry Ward's Robert Elsmere.*

19. Yvonne Ffrench, *Mrs. Gaskell* (Denver, Colorado, 1949), p. 97.
20. Margaret Maison, *The Victorian Vision: Studies in the Religious Novel* (New York, 1961), pp. 1-2.
21. J. Stuart Walters, *Mrs. Humphry Ward, Her Work and Influence* (London, 1912), p. 14.
22. Trevelyan, p. 59.
23. Ibid., p. 61.
24. Ryals, p. xxxviii.
25. *The History of David Grieve* (New York, 1908), p. 109.
26. Ibid., p. 155.
27. Ibid., p. 554.
28. Ibid., pp. viii-ix.
29. Trevelyan, p. 143.
30. "An Italian Opinion of Helbeck of Bannisdale," *American Monthly Review of Reviews* XIX (January 1899): 116.
31. Trevelyan, p. 147.
32. *Helbeck of Bannisdale* (New York, 1910), p. 202.
33. Ibid., p. 228.
34. Ibid., p. 230.
35. Ibid., p. 332.
36. *The Case of Richard Meynell* (New York, 1910), p. 542.
37. Ibid., p. vii.

Chapter Three

1. "*Marcella,* Mrs. Humphry Ward's New Novel on Socialism and Wealth," *Review of Reviews* IX (April 1894): 492.
2. *Marcella* (Boston, 1910), pp. xi-xii.
3. Ibid., p. xviii.
4. Trevelyan, p. 95.
5. *Marcella,* I, 141.
6. Ibid., I, 3.
7. Ibid., I, 46.
8. Ibid., I, 74.
9. Ibid., I, 75-76.
10. Ibid., I, 103.
11. Ibid., II, 131.
12. Ibid., II, 132.
13. Trevelyan, p. 109.
14. Ibid., p. 115.
15. Ibid., p. 116.
16. Ibid., p. 117.
17. "*Sir George Tressady,*" *Century Magazine* LII (May 1896): 28.
18. *Sir George Tressady* (Boston, 1910), p. 218.
19. Trevelyan, p. 112.

20. *The Story of Bessie Costrell* (Boston, 1910), 420.
21. Ibid., p. 456.
22. *Daphne*, or *Marriage à la Mode* (New York, 1909), p. 223.
23. Ibid., p. 123.
24. Ibid., p. 125.
25. Trevelyan, p. 233.
26. *Delia Blanchflower* (New York, 1914), p. 136.

Chapter Four

1. Charles Dudley Warner, ed., *A Library of the World's Best Literature* (New York, 1897), p. 15642.
2. *Miss Bretherton* (Boston, 1910), pp. 223–24.
3. Ibid., p. 240.
4. Trevelyan, p. 168.
5. *A Writer's Recollections*, II, 198.
6. Jill Colaco, "Henry James and Mrs. Humphry Ward: A Misunderstanding," *Notes and Queries* XXIII (September 1976): 409.
7. Ibid.
8. Ibid., p. 410.
9. *A Writer's Recollections*, II, 217.
10. Ibid., II, 114–15.
11. Ibid., II, 223.
12. Stephen Gwynn, "Mrs. Humphry Ward," in *Writers of the Day*, ed. Bertram Christian (London, 1917), pp. 76–77.
13. *Lady Rose's Daughter* (Boston, 1910), p. x.
14. Abel Chevalley, *The Modern English Novel*, translated by Ben Ray Redman (New York, 1925), p. 56.
15. *Lady Rose's Daughter*, p. 131.
16. Ibid., p. 221.
17. Ibid., p. 404.
18. Hamilton W. Mabie, "The Work of Mrs. Humphry Ward," *North American Review* CLXXVI (April 1903): 486–87.
19. Lord David Cecil, *Melbourne* (New York, 1954), p. 72.
20. Ibid., p. 70.
21. *The Marriage of William Ashe* (Boston, 1910), pp. 71–72.
22. Ibid., p. 432.
23. "A Word with Mrs. Humphry Ward," *Blackwood's Edinburgh Magazine* CLXXVII (July 1905): 19.
24. Trevelyan, p. 177.
25. Ibid., p. 206.
26. *Fenwick's Career* (Boston, 1910), pp. 162–63.
27. Ibid., pp. 288–89.
28. Ibid., p. xiv.
29. Ibid., p. 222.

30. Trevelyan, p. 204.
31. *Review of Reviews* XXXVIII (November 1908): 634.
32. *Spectator* CI (October 3, 1908): 506.
33. *Independent* LXV (October 15, 1908): 896.
34. *Nation* XC (April 21, 1910): 402.
35. *Lady Merton, Colonist,* or *Canadian Born* (New York, 1910), pp. 281-82.
36. *New York Times* XVIII (April 6, 1913): 200.
37. *The Coryston Family* (New York, 1913), p. 85.
38. Ibid., pp. 121-22.
39. Ibid., p. 326.
40. Ibid., p. 79.
41. *Spectator* CXI (October 18, 1913): 616.
42. *New York Times* XVIII (October 19, 1913): 563.
43. *Eltham House* (New York, 1915), p. vi.
44. Ibid., p. vii.
45. *A Great Success* (New York, 1916), p. 41.
46. *Saturday Review* CXXI (March 18, 1916): 283.
47. *Boston Transcript,* October 25, 1916, p. 8
48. *Lady Connie* (New York, 1916), pp. 250-51.
49. U. C. Knoepflmacher, "The Rival Ladies: Mrs. Humphry Ward's *Lady Connie* and D. H. Lawrence's *Lady Chatterley's Lover,*" *Victorian Studies* IV (December 1960): 141-58.
50. D. H. Lawrence, "Study of Thomas Hardy," in *Selected Criticism,* ed. Anthony Beal (London, 1955), p. 177.
51. Knoepflmacher, pp. 143-44.
52. Ibid., p. 155.

Chapter Five

1. *England's Effort: Letters to an American Friend* (New York, 1916), p. 12.
2. Trevelyan, p. 269.
3. Ibid., p. 285.
4. *Fields of Victory* (New York, 1919), p. vii.
5. Trevelyan, p. 271.
6. *England's Effort,* p. 37.
7. *Towards the Goal* (New York, 1918), p. vii.
8. Ibid., p. ix.
9. *Fields of Victory,* pp. 13-14.
10. André Malraux, *L'Espoir* (Paris, 1937), pp. 270-71.
11. *The War and Elizabeth,* or *Elizabeth's Campaign* (London, 1918), p. 154.
12. Ibid., p. 201.
13. Ibid., p. 106.

14. Ibid., p. 107.
15. Ibid., p. 144.
16. Ibid., p. 252.
17. *Cousin Philip*, or *Helena* (London, 1919), p. 187.
18. Ibid., p. 47
19. Ibid., p. 51.
20. *Harvest* (New York, 1920), p. 345.
21. *Athenaeum*, May 7, 1920, p. 606.
22. *Bookman* L (February 1920): 629.
23. *London Times Literary Supplement*, November 27, 1919, p. 694.
24. *Dial* LXIV (January 31, 1918): 117.
25. *Boston Transcript*, November 3, 1917, p. 8.
26. *Nation* CVII (October 26, 1918): 592.
27. *Outlook* CXX (November 6, 1918): 380.
28. *Harvest*, p. 235.
29. Ibid., p. 135.
30. Ibid., p. 136.
31. *The Fox*, in *The Portable D. H. Lawrence* (New York, 1961), p. 300.
32. Ibid., p. 305.
33. *A Writer's Recollections*, I, 10, note.
34. Ibid., I, 145-46.
35. Ibid., II, 197.
36. Ibid., II, 234-35.
37. Ibid., II, 242-43.
38. Ibid., II, 244-45.

Chapter Six

1. Enid Huws Jones, *Mrs. Humphry Ward.*
2. William S. Peterson, *Victorian Heretic* (Leicester, England, 1976).
3. Walters, pp. 31-32.
4. Ibid., p. 26.
5. Muriel Harris, "Mrs. Humphry Ward," *Nation* CX (April 3, 1920): 424.
6. Muriel Harris, "Mrs. Humphry Ward," *North American Review* CCXI (June 1920): 819.
7. William Lyon Phelps, *Essays on Modern Novelists* (New York, 1921), p. 91.
8. Lionel Stevenson, *The English Novel, a Panorama* (Boston, 1960), p. 417.
9. Harriet W. Preston, "*Lady Rose's Daughter;* The Novels of Mr. Norris," *Atlantic Monthly* XCI (May 1903): 68-69.

10. C. H. Gaines, "*The Marriage of William Ashe,*" *Harper's Weekly* XLIX (March 18, 1905): 392.
11. William Dean Howells, *Heroines of Fiction* (New York, 1901), p. 273.
12. Jones, p. 155.
13. Ibid., p. 169.
14. Peterson, p. 206.

Selected Bibliography

PRIMARY SOURCES

This list of major works gives American first-edition dates and publishers; where there is considerable discrepancy between American publication and first English editions, the earlier publication data are added. For a complete list of all Mrs. Ward's works, including articles, lectures, introductions, pamphlets, and dramas, see William S. Peterson, *Victorian Heretic: Mrs. Humphry Ward's Robert Elsmere.* Leicester, England: Leicester University Press, 1976.

Amiel's Journal: The Journal Intime of Henri Frederic Amiel, translated with an Introduction by Mrs. Humphry Ward. New York: Brentano's, 1928; London: Macmillan and Company, 1885.

The Case of Richard Meynell. New York: Hurst & Co., 1910.

The Coryston Family. New York: Harper & Brothers, 1913.

Delia Blanchflower. New York: Hearst's International Library Co., 1914.

A Dictionary of Christian Biography, eds. William Smith and Henry Wace. Boston: Little, Brown and Co., 1871, I; London: John Murray, 1880, 1882, 1887, II, III, IV (Mrs. Ward wrote almost two hundred articles).

Eleanor. New York: Harper & Brothers, 1900.

Elizabeth's Campaign. New York: Dodd, Mead and Company, 1918; English title: *The War and Elizabeth.* London: W. Collins Sons & Co., Ltd., 1918.

Eltham House. New York: Hearst's International Library Co., 1915; also New York: Grosset & Dunlap, 1915.

England's Effort: Letters to an American Friend. New York: Charles Scribner's Sons, 1916.

Fenwick's Career. New York: Harper & Brothers, 1906.

Fields of Victory. New York: Charles Scribner's Sons, 1919.

A Great Success. New York: Hearst's International Library Co., 1916.

Harvest. New York: Dodd, Mead and Co., 1920.

Helbeck of Bannisdale. New York: The Macmillan Co., 1898.

Helene. New York: Dodd, Mead and Co., 1919; English title: *Cousin Philip.* London: W. Collins Sons & Co., Ltd., 1919.

The History of David Grieve. New York: The Macmillan Co., 1892.

Lady Connie. New York: Hearst's International Library Co., 1916.

Lady Merton, Colonist. New York: Doubleday, Page & Co., 1910; English title: *Canadian Born.* London: Smith, Elder & Co., 1910.
Lady Rose's Daughter. New York: Harper & Brothers, 1903 (also Grosset & Dunlap, 1903).
Marcella. 2 vols. New York: The Macmillan Co., 1894.
Marriage à la Mode. New York: Doubleday, Page & Co., 1909; English title: *Daphne.* London: Cassell, 1909.
The Marriage of William Ashe. New York: Harper & Brothers, 1905.
The Mating of Lydia. Garden City, New York: Doubleday, Page & Co., 1913.
Milly and Olly. New York: Doubleday, Page & Co., 1907; London: Macmillan and Company, 1884.
Miss Bretherton. New York: J. W. Lovell Company, 1888; London: Macmillan and Company, 1884.
"Missing." New York: Dodd, Mead and Co., 1917.
Robert Elsmere. New York: The Macmillan Co., 1888 (many other editions; latest, a paperback, edited by Clyde DeL. Ryals, published by University of Nebraska Press, 1967).
Sir George Tressady. New York: The Macmillan Co., 1896.
The Story of Bessie Costrell. New York: The Macmillan Co., 1895.
The Testing of Diana Mallory. New York: Harper & Brothers, 1908.
Towards the Goal. New York: Charles Scribner's Sons, 1918.
A Writer's Recollections. 2 vols. New York: Harper & Brothers, 1918.

SECONDARY SOURCES

1. Books

CECIL, LORD DAVID. *Melbourne.* New York: Grosset & Dunlap, 1954. Excellent verification of Mrs. Ward's authenticity in *The Marriage of William Ashe.*
CHEVALLEY, ABEL. *The Modern English Novel,* trans. Ben Ray Redman. New York: Alfred A. Knopf, 1925. Good foreign evaluation of Mrs. Ward as interpreter of her nation and period.
CROSS, WILBUR L. *The Development of the English Novel.* New York: The Macmillan Co., 1922. Excellent comparison of George Eliot, Henry James, Mrs. Ward.
DAVIES, HORTON. *A Mirror of the Ministry in Modern Novels.* New York: Oxford University Press, 1959. Places *Robert Elsmere* in its special genre.
ELIOT, THOMAS STEARNS. *The Family Reunion.* New York: Harcourt, Brace & World, Inc., 1939. Valuable comparative work.
FFRENCH, YVONNE. *Mrs. Gaskell.* Denver: Alan Swallow, 1949. Perceptive study of Mrs. Gaskell that sheds light on Mrs. Ward.

GWYNN, STEPHEN. "Mrs. Humphry Ward," in *Writers of the Day*, ed. Bertram Christian. London: Nesbet & Co., Ltd., 1917. A thorough, fair evaluation of many of Mrs. Ward's novels.

HOWELLS, WILLIAM DEAN. *Heroines of Fiction*. New York: Harper & Brothers, 1901. Establishes Mrs. Ward's rank and gives insight into the differences between American and English fiction.

JONES, ENID HUWS. *Mrs. Humphry Ward*. New York: St. Martin's Press, 1973. Presents hitherto hidden personal details and emphasizes her social reform work.

LAWRENCE, D. H. *The Ladybird: The Fox: The Captain's Doll*. London: M. Seeker, 1925; *The Fox*, in *The Portable D. H. Lawrence*. New York: The Viking Press, 1961. A rewrite of Mrs. Ward's last novel.

KNOEPFLMACHER, U. C. *Religious Humanism and the Victorian Novel: George Eliot, Walter Pater, and Samuel Butler*. Princeton, New Jersey: Princeton University Press, 1965. Brief but perceptive analysis of Mrs. Ward's literary and philosophical relationship to George Eliot and Walter Pater.

MAISON, MARGARET M. *The Victorian Vision: Studies in the Religious Novel*. New York: Sheed & Ward, 1961. Comprehensive tracing of the role of religion in the development of the novel.

PETERSON, WILLIAM S. *Victorian Heretic: Mrs. Humphry Ward's Robert Elsmere*. Leicester, England: Leicester University Press, 1976. Suggests Mrs. Ward struggled with a religious dichotomy unresolved by her religious fiction. Contains a definitive bibliography.

PHELPS, WILLIAM LYON. *Essays on Modern Novelists*. New York: The Macmillan Co., 1921. Witty but confused condemnation of Mrs. Ward's art.

RYALS, CLYDE DE., ed. "Introduction by the Editor," Mrs. Humphry Ward. *Robert Elsmere*. Lincoln: University of Nebraska Press, 1967. Argues the novel's contemporaneity.

STEVENSON, LIONEL. *The English Novel, a Panorama*. Boston: Houghton Mifflin Co., 1960. Reputable but unsympathetic evaluation.

TREVELYAN, JANET PENROSE. *The Life of Mrs. Humphry Ward*. New York: Dodd, Mead and Co., 1923. Informative biography with emphasis on career rather than personal life.

WALTERS, J. STUART. *Mrs. Humphry Ward, Her Work and Influence*. London: Kegan Paul, Trench, Trubner & Co., Ltd., 1912. Sympathetic analysis emphasizing Mrs. Ward's place in her period rather than her art.

WARNER, CHARLES DUDLEY, ed. *A Library of the World's Best Literature*. 45 vols. New York: The International Society, 1897. Accurate contemporary evaluation of Mrs. Ward's work.

2. Periodicals

BEYSCHLAG, PROFESSOR. "A German Criticism of Robert Elsmere." *Review of Reviews* I (April 1889): 397. Representative of the international theological discussion of the novel.

COLACO, JILL. "Henry James and Mrs. Humphry Ward: A Misunderstanding." *Notes and Queries* XXIII (September 1976): 408–10. Corrects erroneous impression of Henry James's influence on *Eleanor.*

DALGLEISH, DORIS N. "Faith and Doubt in Victorian Literature." *Contemporary Review* (February 1948): 106–12. A modern evaluation of *Robert Elsmere* within its genre.

GILMAN, LAWRENCE. "The Mind of Mrs. Humphry Ward." *North American Review* CCIX (February 1919): 267–71. A scathing review of *A Writer's Recollections.*

GLADSTONE, WILLIAM E. "*Robert Elsmere* and the Battle of Belief." *Nineteenth Century* XXIII (May 1888): 766–88. Significance due entirely to the fame of the author.

HARRIS, MURIEL. "Mrs. Humphry Ward." *Nation* CX (April 3, 1920): 424–25. Eulogistic emphasis on her role as the last of her age.

———. "Mrs. Humphry Ward." *North American Review* CCXI (June 1920): 818–25. Emphasis on her role as a propagandist.

KNOEPFLMACHER, U. C. "The Rival Ladies: Mrs. Humphry Ward's *Lady Connie* and D. H. Lawrence's *Lady Chatterley's Lover.*" *Victorian Studies* IV (December 1960): 141–58. Detailed comparison and intriguing discussion of Mrs. Ward's influence.

LEWIS, NAOMI. "The Immortelles of the Book World—Mrs. Humphry Ward." *New Statesman & Nation* XXXIV (August 23, 1947): 152. Sympathetic analysis.

MABIE, HAMILTON W. "The Work of Mrs. Humphry Ward." *North American Review* CLXXVI (April 1903): 481–89. Excellent discussion of both the didactic and the artistic elements of her work.

MAGNUS, LAURIE. "Mrs. Humphry Ward." *Living Age* XIV (January 1902): 103–107. Balanced criticism.

"*Marcella,* Mrs. Humphry Ward's New Novel on Socialism and Wealth." *Review of Reviews* IX (April 1894): 492–99. Good example of early reviews.

MARINET, J. VAN LOENEN. "Yet Another View of *Robert Elsmere,*" reprinted from *De Gids.* In *Review of Reviews* II (August 1890): 233. Enthusiastic appreciation from the Netherlands.

MARCIN, F. S. "*Robert Elsmere* Fifty Years After." *Contemporary Review* CLVI (August 1939): 196–202. Limited to an evaluation of the religious issues.

MIVART, ST. GEORGE. "Another Catholic's View of *Helbeck of Ban-*

nisdale." *Nineteenth Century* XLIV (October 1898): 641-55. Careful, favorable analysis.

"Mrs. Humphry Ward's Art," from *The Speaker.* In *Living Age* XXVII (May 1905): 186-90. Analysis of her craftsmanship versus her art.

"Mrs. Ward's Latest Novel." *Nation* LXXX (April 27, 1905): 336. Good review of *The Marriage of William Ashe.*

"Notable Fiction of Spring and Summer." *American Monthly Review of Reviews* XXXI (December 1905): 755-56. Praise of her intelligent craftsmanship.

"The Old Saloon." *Blackwood's Edinburgh Magazine* CVI (March 1892): 455-74. Reluctant praise, quizzical evaluation of first two novels.

PRESTON, HARRIET S. *"Lady Rose's Daughter;* The Novels of Mr. Norris." *Atlantic Monthly* XCI (May 1903): 687-92. Realistic appraisal from American viewpoint.

"*Robert Elsmere* by Mrs. Humphry Ward." *Quarterly Review* CLXVII (October 1888): 273-302. Commendatory of her style, condemnatory of her theology; the review she felt compelled to answer.

SERGÉ, CARLO. "An Italian Opinion of *Helbeck of Bannisdale.*" *American Monthly Review of Reviews* XIX (January 1899): 116. Pertinent foreign reaction.

"The Victorian Solitude," from *Nation.* In *Living Age* CCXCIX (December 1918): 680-82. Critical of all things Victorian.

Index